Falling from Grace

FALLING FROM
—GRACE—
MY EARLY YEARS IN BALLET

—UNA FLETT—

CANONGATE
EDINBURGH
1981

First published in 1981 by
Canongate Publishing Ltd.
17 Jeffrey Street, Edinburgh

© 1981 Una Flett

ISBN 0 86241 011 8 (cased)

The author and publishers acknowledge the financial assistance
of the Scottish Arts Council in the
publication of this book

Typeset by Hugh K. Clarkson & Sons Ltd.,
Young Street, West Lothian
Printed in Scotland by Thomson Litho Ltd., East Kilbride

Introduction

This book is the fulfilment of a promise made in my 'teens that I would some time write a book about dancers and dancing. At the time I was crazy about ballet, in the way that young people in those passionate one-dimensional years are crazy about sport or acting or machines or horse-riding or the other sex, and generally intend to be a dazzling success in the mania of their choice. I was not only crazy about ballet, but spent most of my waking hours actively engaged in it, a full-time ballet student.

I wanted to write a book about its magic and its extraordinary beauty, and about the curious fact that dancers always made me think of nuns. Underneath the trappings of stage and excitement, make-up and costume, was an austerity, an obedience to ritual discipline, and a rather terrifying single-mindedness, which could only be equated with a religious quest. But even in my infatuated 'teens, some vague protest stirred from time to time, and occasionally a faint questioning as to whether this sublime love-object was truly worth the sacrifice. This I also wanted to write about.

As it turned out, it was I who had feet of clay, not the idol. After not much more than two years on the professional stage I quit, disillusioned about my own talent and defeated by the toughness of the life. It was like the break-up of a love affair, and took a long, long time to heal.

What I have written still has dancing as its main theme, particularly how it figured in my life from five to sixteen as the source of an amazing joy which is probably unrepeatable. From then till I gave up at the age of twenty it gradually lost its lustre, something

I would choose to forget but which is in fact the heart of the matter. For this story is really about someone reluctant to grow up. I have tried to describe the state of almost permanent romance in which an adolescent sees the world and the rather stunning disillusions which follow.

Dancers have a particularly hard time in weathering this progress (I speak for girls). By their exertions and their desire to remain sylph-like and adrogynous they actually mature physically several years later than other girls. The life they lead, like the convent, is remote and cut off from everyday concerns. They usually show very little interest in anything outside it. It is a Peter Pan world, but one of incredible harshness.

The rest of the world, as I often suspected when I was still 'inside', is too fascinating a place to ignore, and I have few regrets about leaving the ballet. But still there remains a sense of something magical glimpsed and lost, and a twinge of heartache that perfection is not for most of us.

Una Flett
Edinburgh 1981

Early Years

Life started out too pleasantly for me. My first impressions are full of light and colour, for I was born in India in the early 1930s, the third child of a district commissioner in the Indian Civil Service, which meant that we lived in a succession of bungalows surrounded by wide gardens and cared for by a dozen servants. By the time my memory starts to function clearly, we were in Ranchi, then summer capital of Bihar, and I am told that it was a beautiful place. My recollections are piecemeal, silver and flowered garlands thrown round our necks when my father went on official visits, the brilliant colours of women's saris and the inches of glass bangles they wore on their arms, flicking them out of the way with a tinkly click as they worked; flowers that flopped from blossoming trees; a shrine on the top of a little hill known as Tagore's Hill; a plant whose leaves snapped shut like a book when you ran your finger down its stem; swarms of baby frogs when the rains came. And always a sense of infinite horizons, infinite time. A big, beautiful world in which I was small and very safe, and in which each day ended with the lovely sensation of being put to bed in the airy enclosure of a mosquito net.

My parents were the kindest in the world. But even their love for their children did not contest the system, which was to send small children back to England to be educated away from the bad effects of the climate and the socially dubious possibility of mixing with Anglo-Indian children. I can see no reason why schools could not have been started up in the hills, where the climate is beautiful. But the system decreed otherwise, and so at a very early age we left our home and were sent to boarding school. My older sister and brother went first and I followed two years later, aged five.

Generations of India-born children have undergone this traumatic separation. Read Rudyard Kipling, read Rumer Godden, the tale of childish despair at being abandoned is the same. Ask any British adult who started life in the unnatural paradise of the Empire about their homecoming, and the answer is always in terms of shock and terrible heartache. 'My eldest daughter has never forgiven me,' said an elderly memsahib to me recently. Her daughter must by this time be approaching sixty.

Even at the age of five I knew that the gravy-brown hideousness of a private boarding-school was a kind of outrage to life. Along with agonies of home-sickness went the sense that a whole world of bright sensations had been suddenly eclipsed, that singing about 'All things bright and beautiful' in an ugly red-brick chapel, dressed in a navy gaberdine trailing dejectedly below my knees was as grotesque as praising freedom from a prison. If I had been more of a fighter I would have kicked and raged, but instead my lower lip was always quivering and on the point of collapsing completely into sobs of unhappiness. It did not help that the headmistress, an awesome woman with a rough red complexion and iron-grey hair had a disgust of weeping which made me an immediate pariah.

'I don't like little girls who cry,' she said insistently, as though when I parted from my mother and wept I had somehow soiled myself and threatened to spread pollution to her as well. Aunt Clare, as she styled herself, was the wife of a retired colonel, and my guess is that the 'home school for children of parents abroad' was simply a rather tedious expedient to hang onto a large house and grounds which might otherwise have been too costly. My guess is, too, that she had been made to carry the can. Uncle Geoff, her husband, figured only as a large affable lump sprawled behind a spread of newspaper at breakfast, and there was also a fat and languid grown-up daughter who swanned in and out of the scene, but took no part in the running of the school.

Conscientious in her duties, Aunt Clare personally scrubbed

the 'little ones' nightly in the communal bathroom, enveloped in a red rubber apron which suggested she was performing some unpleasant clinical task. Frightened out of my wits as I was, I seemed to stick out from the rest by some kind of self-assertion, gaining the nickname 'Me'—presumably because I made heavy use of the pronoun. She scared me silly, yet in the absence of any other mother-figure she became one—very large and very grim but nonetheless the person to whom I must, willy-nilly, attach myself.

It was like trying to find comfort from a whin-bush growing on a jagged rock, after the pampered lotus-eating years in India. For there I had had, not only my own mother, but like all India-reared children my ayah, who used to dress me up in one of her spare saris, and took me down to gossip and chat with the other servants in the middle of the day when my mother was resting. Ayah, who was elderly and humorous and patient, would sit me down on the sagging string bed in the dimness of her hut, and feed me titbits from the food she and the others cooked on open braziers in the space outside. Though it may have reflected an indefensible system of ruler and ruled, I think the fondness shown me by all our servants was genuine, stemming from second-generation loyalty to our family in general. Many of them were the sons of fathers who had served my father when he first came to Bihar. I only know that, in sentimental mood, it is not only the constant stream of gifts that I remember—bazaar sweetmeats, glass bangles by the dozen, a miniature sari of my own, even a tiny violin—but all the patience, the readiness to play with me, the comforting in times of distress. In India, I was lapped around with permissive love and attention. At boarding school I was suddenly shivering in the wind of indifference and up against a thousand rules on which I barked my shins uncomprehending, good conduct marks being stripped off left and right and making me the shame of the dormitory.

And in between there had been the fretful interlude of homecoming, a sea voyage with my mother who taught me to read to quieten my itch to make sense of the printed word, a reunion with my sister and brother during a cold grey Easter holiday spent in Dublin with our Irish grandparents. They were not pleased at this intrusion of a younger whiny sister on their scene. My sister, in fact, adopted a policy of ignoring me completely and kept it up with remarkable thoroughness during the two years we were at boarding school together. The age gap of four and a half years had been, in any case, immeasurably widened by her experiences of English acculturation. By the time we met up she was safely buttoned into the coping, ostensibly emotionless reserve which spelt adjustment to the no-nonsense atmosphere of school. A more sturdy character than myself, she even managed to enjoy certain aspects of our incarceration, such as horse-riding, and was not by this time, if she ever had been, overwhelmed by the towering authority figure of Aunt Clare. My brother, mid-way in age between us, had by this time left the 'home school' (a title of insulting irony) and had gone off to prep school so we only saw him in the holidays. He seemed to accept me much more easily, being even then a kind and protective little boy. But at school I had no protector and was rottenly equipped to fend for myself.

Sentimental though it may sound, it was in fact the arts, first in the form of music and then dance, which first held out some shreds of comfort in this dreary place, as much to do with the personalities of the people involved as to my own natural inclinations. Miss Wrightson, who came to give us piano lessons, could not replace the sun-filled chattering ease of India, but she did bring a sort of quietness, an unhurried feeling, and a singleness of concentration, all wonderfully in contrast with the banging and shoving of herd life. She was a gentle green-and-brown woman, always dressed in a suit and blouse of those colours, tall and angular with a skin which already had a soft, folded look more to do with inner resignation than actual age. The day I went for my first music lesson, in a small poky room somewhere near the boiler-house and the cloak-rooms, I told her I could already play tunes on the piano. 'Indeed?' she said, surprised. 'Well, play me something.' So I did—tunes that I had spent engrossed hours picking out on the piano in our drawing room in India, with its swathes of blue net curtains and a ceiling fan being idly turned by the punkah-wallah slumped in a corner twitching the cord with his big toe. I was on familiar and happy ground.

Miss Wrightson was impressed. 'That was very good,' she said gravely. It was the first piece of affirmation I had received since I got to that place. 'Now we shall learn in a different way.' So we embarked on Book One of the series which started with a little tune: 'Buy a broom, buy a broom, buy a broom and sweep the room.' And later came the fun of putting left and right hands together, and I was away.

Dancing came differently, in one burst of revelation. One day a group of dancers came to the school and gave a performance. It sounds so unlikely, in that wilderness of broken pencil points and over-cooked liver and lost wellington boots, that I've since wondered at an event which seems to belong more to present-day attempts to broaden the curriculum than the sparse utilitarianism of our school. However it came about the fact remains, there was this performance, of which I can remember no details, only a dazzle of brightness and a gaiety which spelt, for as long as it lasted, a total reprieve from the anxious gloom in which I habitually plodded round. It was true after all. Colour, excitement, joy was not something lost forever. When the curtain came down I knew it was only a veil. I might still be on the wrong side, but it *did* exist—magic and happiness and beautiful people. I loved them and what they did with a great burst of fervent love.

The follow-up to the visit was a more tepid experience. Dancing classes were started at school, and my debut as a performer took the form of skipping through the rockery in the school garden, dressed in a purple crepe paper skirt leading five other flower fairies in some outdoor pageant called 'Through the Crocus Tunnel'—a fairly typical initiation into dance for a small girl.

And thereafter I have no very clear memories of that school except those associated with my attempts to follow a path of

5

cautious virtue, being 'good' in the totally negative way of
abstaining from any action that could lead to trouble. It makes
humiliating remembering—so much more satisfying to have been
able to look back on a record of infant rebellion, being a 'bad girl',
instead of that most pallid of school-girl story-book characters.
However, I was only six, some small excuse for giving way to
fear.

Aunt Clare, who was a shrewd enough judge of character—if
one is into the business of treating small children like adults being
assessed for a job—was well aware of the difference between
correctness and something more positive. She told the assembled
school as she somewhat grudgingly gave me a badge for good
conduct that I 'followed a little road of my own', and showed little
sign of co-operating with others. She was right. I had no team
spirit. I hadn't made many friends, and even took a perverse
pleasure in snubbing one warm-hearted lovable girl who,
amazingly, persisted in trying to share her toys and her friendship
with me. I remember her hurt angry little face, and my own
compulsive rejection of all the nice things she was offering—that
we could take it in turns to push her doll's pram, that her
beautiful baby doll with hand-knitted woolly clothes could be
'shared'. Why my mother had left me so completely unequipped
with even the few toys we were allowed to bring to school I don't
know. I had no doll (in India I had had eight, which were all given
away when I left), and without a doll one was simply excluded
from the play-club of little girls. It is true I had Angela, a stiff toy
fluff-covered dog who presided over my pyjamas and comforted
me a little at bed-time. But, hopeless at looking after what I did
possess, the rest of my few belongings—playing-cards in a green
leather case with my name in gold letters, a few books, a set of
crayons—had soon disappeared from my locker and all I seemed
to have left were one or two lumps of plasticine, brown in colour
like the linoleum and the furniture, from all the colours having
got mixed together.

Being permanently miserable tends to bring out unpleasant
little monsters in the psyche. I started to develop a strong aptitude

for telling lies—'fibs', as they were called when detected—and, even more unpleasant, a tendency to bully children still more defenceless than myself. But the real flip-side to that good-conduct button was the never-ending fantasy of vengeance which I created night after night as I lay trying to get to sleep. The object of my hatred was, of course, Aunt Clare whom my imagination brought to humiliation and pitiful cringing in as many horrible ways as I could devise. This fantasy, indeed, outlasted my days at the school, and would recur long after life had changed for the better, as though in some way I had ingested this terrifying woman and had periodically to try and deal with a stubborn phantom that lived on inside me. Worse still, as an adult with two small children, I would, in moments of maternal anger feel myself, to my horror, becoming Aunt Clare, a horrible over-sized grim figure. . . .

In reality, she died the summer that war broke out, of cancer. My enemy had been suffering from a fatal disease. Perhaps I had done her to death too often in fantasy for the news of her actual demise to have much effect. Or perhaps it was simply that, with my mother home for the holidays, and school life thereby pushed as far from my thoughts as possible, the fact hardly registered at the time. It certainly made little emotional impact. It is only in looking back that this additional grimness of a dying authority figure gets added into the picture of the school. But I cannot help wondering if part of my terror of her was not because, at some intuitive level, I picked up some sense of her hopeless condition. Children's perceptions are sharp, and it was a fear of annihilation that I felt through this woman, who had wiped out the child I had been in India and replaced her with a creature more or less permanently ashamed and guilty. Aunt Clare must have been exercising some terrible piece of stoic control over herself to carry out her duties. Small wonder if some of the need to suppress her own deep fears got projected onto us.

The queries which her death raised about the future of my sister and myself, and whether we should return to the boarding school, were made much more urgent by the threat of war. When it seemed certain that it was going to be declared, my mother had to revise her plans which had been, as always, to return to my father in India, for the school was in an area in the south earmarked as a danger zone. There was now no question of sending us back, and we stayed put where we were, in Moffat, a quiet Scottish border town, set in a charming landscape of rolling hills.

For me personally that was the luckiest break in my life. I was in a somewhat wretched state, with some kind of glandular infection in my neck, and a tendency to have violent nightmares which had me sleepwalking round the house and once into the garden. I still told lies more naturally than I spoke the truth and occasionally stole things, and if I had returned to that detested school I might have been quite severely damaged. On the other hand, there is always the possibility that I might have emerged toughened to a degree I shall never achieve now. On balance, I prefer things the way they happened, and ascribe such resilience as I have to the years of quiet undemanding family life which replaced the boarding school experience.

War-Time

We stayed in Moffat because that is where, for reasons of family connections and sentiment, my mother always returned for holidays. We still had a few elderly cousins and a frail, spiky, white-haired great-grandmother there, whose handsome beaked profile, black walking stick and snapping dark eyes put over as strong a message of indomitable will as her stooped back and little twisted feet in lumpy patent-leather shoes proclaimed her fragility. I used to want to sit on her knee and inevitably got the reply: 'You can't, because I've got a bone in my leg', one of those futile adult jokes that I would puzzle away at for hidden subtlety.

The town itself received the impact of wartime in the form of British troops, sections of the exiled Polish army and a few civilian Polish refugee families, Clydeside evacuees, and one momentous bomb-dropping episode when a fleeing German bomber off-loaded into a field on the outskirts. Three large craters and a dead sheep was the result. Moffat had genuinely been bombed.

We moved, the three of us, becoming four in the holidays when my brother came back from school, from one rented house or part-house approximately every six months. Our ages at the outbreak of war were eleven-and-a-half, ten and seven—not a popular age-range with landladies. And although we were quite depressingly well-behaved, I suppose there was inevitably a certain amount of noise and mess. My sister was the most spirited in her defiance of lodgers' rules, finding keys for cupboards or rooms that were meant to be kept locked, using objects that were

9

sancrosanct and generally following her incredible detective curiosity for nosing and observing.

She and I aggravated each other like pepper rubbed into a raw and itching surface. Since we had to share a bedroom till she was seventeen, we had six long years in which to sharpen our different natures on each other. Jill was a pragmatist, firmly rooted into the real world by her excellent powers of observation and her curiosity about natural history. As to feelings, she kept these well hidden behind a stance of devastatingly accurate criticism, and had nothing but intolerance for my emotional outbursts and love of histrionics. She made me look endlessly silly, with my imaginings and posturing and love of dressing up, and I expect I made her look stolid and reserved and unentertaining. In fact, despite the shared bedroom, we inhabited almost separate worlds, much of mine inside my own head, and our points of contact were almost always in the form of argument or wrangling of some sort. In these encounters I inevitably got the worst, no match, with my fatally quick temper, for her formidable sarcastic deflating. Yet every now and then she would throw herself into one of my ploys with a sudden burst of enthusiasm. I had written a carol one Christmas, and she inscribed it most beautifully on a piece of parchment which she turned into a decorative scroll, complete with scarlet ribbons and seal, and this we presented proudly to our mother.

As for my brother, he also teased me to distraction, as everyone did since I was so unbelievably easy to rile. But his teasing was different, lacking the fine edge of implied dismissal which was so galling about my sister's. And often he was kind, comforting me with remarkable sweetness, even getting up in the middle of the night to massage my legs which sometimes ached intolerably with those mysterious pains called 'growing pains'.

My mother was, of course, faced with the problem of finding another school for us, and it seemed a happy coincidence that a new school had just been started by—once again—an ex-army officer and his wife, to which many of Moffat's genteel parents, probably faced with the same problem as my mother, sent their children. It was a pleasant enough establishment, housed in a rambling white-walled building known as the Old Rectory. Classes were small, everybody knew everybody, and life proceeded calmly for all of two terms. Mr Garth, the headmaster, was a large, foxy, slightly flashy man with a broad handle-bar moustache, a certain magnetism of personality, and a variable temper. But as one of the juniors I seldom saw him except at morning prayers where he sometimes looked so thunderous that I had the distinct impression he wanted to hurl his little prayer-book at our assembled shining morning faces, instead of mumbling through the collect for the day, or whatever it was that he read out.

His wife was a sweet-faced woman, slightly anxious, with wispy sandy hair knotted back in a bun. Poor woman, she had reason to be anxious. The school closed very suddenly after those promising first two terms with a scandal that rocked the town. Mr Garth had run away to London with one of his prefects—leaving the head-girl collapsed with the shock of rejection. In London, so the story goes, he tried to gate-crash an exclusive regimental club by masquerading as one of its officers, at which point the law took over. It turned out that his wife was not his wife at all, and furthermore, that he had a 'silver plate in his head' from a wound in the First World War. This picturesque affliction accounted for his eccentric behaviour. In other words, Mr Garth was to some degree insane.

We were all back to square one. Genteel Moffat then sent its daughters and its small pre-prep school sons to yet another newly-started school, which during the brief period of Garth's triumph used to be seen trailing its entire quota of seven pupils rather forlornly for walks in the town. But with the lucky break of that scandal it mushroomed overnight. It grew and prospered and has never looked back. However, at this point we parted company with the crowd. My mother, exasperated with private schools, decided quite rightly that we would do better under state education, and sent us to the local academy. There we got good solid grounding in the three Rs and went on to perform respectably in public examinations, whereas the pupils of that other school, although they wore a lovely red and beige uniform (which I envied) and learnt to ride and dance, had an abyssmal track record when it came to the sterner aspects of education.

My mother's decision did not make her life any easier. Deviation is always questionable, not to say downright damning, and to stand out against the consensus of opinion in a small cliquey place must have required strong convictions and considerable courage. One Moffat matron was heard to say that *she* did not pay taxes so that Mrs Russell could educate her children for nothing.

However, much to the credit of the spurned headmistress, she buried whatever offended feelings she may have had and agreed to let myself and my sister take dancing classes with her girls. And it was here that my dancing life was pushed forward a little further, for Mrs Gardner had herself been a professional dancer, and she knew something about ballet training. Her classes, to begin with, were way beyond anything my sister and I could cope with. For one thing, we were quite amazingly stiff. I fortunately did not feel particularly self-conscious about it. I was so thoroughly pleased to be dancing that the fact that I couldn't 'shoulder my leg'—take hold of the instep of one foot and extend the leg at arm's length—without buckling both knees didn't worry me. In any case, I soon started to loosen up. But my sister, being older and less enthusiastic, did not, and gave up after a few terms.

This stiffness was, I am sure, much less to do with any physical deficiency than with our sadly unconfident attitude towards the physical world. Like so many bright, wordy families, as long as we were juggling things round in our minds we were all right—more than all right—distinctly cocky and conceited. But we held our bodies in tight, cautious little packets, documented in one terrible photograph of the three of us looking like some infant line-up for the firing squad. For myself, it is one of the many conflicting themes I've lived out, a struggle between a love of wide, free movement and, equally strong, the self-saving impulse to draw in small, tight, motionless, like an animal that lies low till danger is passed.

It was at Mrs Gardner's that I first learnt to single out a special form of dancing called ballet, for she had one pupil who was already outstanding, an older girl with a refined haughty profile and a great deal of conscious stage charm, and it was on her slender arched feet that I first became aware of the lure of pink satin point-shoes, a lure curiously compounded of purity and eroticism. Like many powerfully charged impressions, this one did not immediately make itself felt. I had no wish then to emulate beautiful Biddy poised on her arched pink feet, and was blissfully happy stamping and clicking my heels as a Polish peasant girl in one of Mrs Gardner's school shows, which included a piece about a Polish wedding, presumably inspired by the exiles whose picturesque uniformed presence was making itself felt in the town.

I have the memory of this event somewhat confused with the dazzle and excitement of that first show I'd watched at boarding school. But I do remember that my happiness was full to overflowing because of the sensual intoxication of wearing a pair of soft red leather boots as part of my peasant costume. They fitted in well to my current obsession, for as if to make up for those two years of solid drabness I had an appetite for bright red that was insatiable. Scarves, boxes, buttons, pencils, notebooks, mittens—anything and everything that was red I coveted. But the boots, alas, were only hired and had to be returned.

As well as Mrs Gardner's ballet classes, I learnt 'Highland dancing' with an itinerant teacher which was also fun, and I was always eager to jump up and show off my neat skill in dancing a sword dance without kicking the crossed blades out of alignment. But during the Moffat years dancing was only one of many matters jostling for attention. Life was extremely busy. There was bicycling and learning to swim in an ice-cold burn, making perfume out of flower petals (they rotted and stank), and trying out in play a selection of occupations—school-teaching, editing a newspaper, running a housing agency, being a famous author. There were tense shifts of allegiance with other small girls, minor skirmishes with a gang of 'big boys' who tried to knock us off our bikes or bust up a little hut some of us had built among the rhodedendron bushes in the Hydro woods, a marvellous sylvan playground in the grounds of what had once been an enormous hydropathic hotel. There were old ladies to visit, some of whom had wonderful relics of their own youth to play with, like dolls dressed in beautiful embroidered and lace-frilled dresses and cloaks trimmed with swans' down.

And there was dreaming—day-dreaming, I mean. I did a lot of that, as well as reading quantities of fairy-tales and myths. I wrote poetry, puzzled about eternity till my head swam slightly, and speculated endlessly about people, sometimes simply using them as fodder for imaginary dramas, at others more directly up against the extraordinary fact that everyone was a different 'me'. And what, I wanted endlessly to know, did it *feel* like to be that different personality? What was it like to be, for example, a member of one of the Polish refugee families, owning nothing but the clothes they were wearing? Or the sad, minor key lady with rugged cheekbones who, my sister said, wanted to make a suicide pact with my mother in the event of a German invasion? 'I wish I could be inside other people's heads', I once said to my mother. She reacted very sharply against this, but not very explicitly. I got the impression she thought it was a meddlesome unwholesome notion.

There were also piano lessons, conducted individually, and singing lessons taken in a group with a rather lugubrious, soulful young woman whom I tried to convince myself was pretty (it was very important that people should be pretty or handsome, although curiously enough at that stage my own unquestionable podgy plain-ness didn't matter). She took voice training, particularly her own, very seriously and tried to get us infant chirpers to produce our notes with correct attention to breathing and diaphragm control. I didn't like this monotonous approach to singing. It was far better fun to band round the piano at home with my brother and sister and have a sing-song, my mother accompanying. We were not, to my great present regret, one of those families where it was a natural activity to pick up a musical

14

instrument and make collective music, but from time to time this urge to sing our way through Scots folk-songs, old English airs, and a few Irish songs did come upon us, and it always gave a rousing sense of solidarity.

After the progression of moves from one touch-me-not domestic interior to the next, we landed up for our final eighteen months in Moffat in a place where such freedoms as family sing-songs and perfume factories could take place. I can only remember one row royal with Mrs Howitt, our last landlady, over some outrage to her home which she would not stand for. Most of the time, this splendid old lady, a minister's widow with too much snap and sparkle by far for her late husband's calling, was a jolly, bustling friend hampered only by appalling deafness. Occasionally, she too would take to the piano, pounding the keyboard with her vigorous plump old arms while she leant back and sang in a leery voice, with many accompanying winks and nods, music-hall songs all about pale moonlight and meeting nice girls in the park. I thought her performance was smashing.

As well as being deaf, she was stout and had feet that bulged with bunions. But she could, when she tried, make herself look exceedingly smart. Her fearsomely corseted figure, which felt like hitting against a barrel if one came in contact, was on Sundays crammed into a tight black suit with beaded lapels. Her poor feet were squeezed into close-fitting black shoes, her white curls gleamed under a black hat, and her mouth was made up with a bright dash of scarlet. My mother admired all this whole-heartedly, sticking up for Mrs Howitt, corsets and all, in the face of our jokes. My mother did not like free-floating fat. Any shape, she felt, was improved by a bit of tailoring.

But when my sister was fifteen we had to leave this house which had acquired the feel of home, even including Mrs Howitt's odious yapping plume-tailed pekinese who occasionally messed in our bedroom. Jill had come to the end of Moffat Academy, at that time a junior secondary with no final senior years. Education demanded that we move somewhere, and the somewhere turned out to be Edinburgh, where my grandfather had long before taken his medical degree (prize finalist of his year) and where my sister had already decided to follow in his footsteps—though when the time came rather deliberately avoiding the search for peculiar distinction.

Edinburgh

How to track back into Edinburgh? It is not easy, for Edinburgh is a place that I have never truly discovered. It emerged piecemeal round me simply as the place where life took up again after we left Moffat, neither surpassingly strange, nor growing warm with real familiarity or a sense of belonging. We had no friends or relatives here, in fact the only reason for being in the place at all was simply to go to school.

And as we started so have I, at least, carried on through most of my life here, in spite of the friendships I've had and the homes I've lived in or made. The thirty and more years are broken by two main absences, one in my 'teens when I was dancing in Paris, and another in my twenties when my husband and I moved to the West Highlands where he lost his life in a drowning accident. The return from both these absences, particularly the second as a widow with two young children, underlined for me the fact that Edinburgh is not a kind place to return to with anything less than a triumphal re-entry. Moreover, it states its decided preference for people whose social label and function is sharply and easily categorised, and their antecedents well established through family and school connections. It requires peoples' masks to be clear and decisive and in no danger of slipping, itself as a town the most beautiful and dignified and possibly empty mask of all.

But on both my returns I was without a mask; coming back from France to give up dancing, I was abandoning the identity I had grown up with in Edinburgh. As for being a widow, it is a kind of null social category. And so I think that my sense of being an alien and an interloper in the nearest thing I have to a home town stems from this feeling that it has no tolerance or place for people in transition, flux, precariousness. Whether it is worse than any other city in this respect, I do not know for certain, but I suspect so. For it is a place of massive settledness. Festivals and international conferences and the growth of the university notwithstanding, it has never acquired the feel of comings and goings, of movement and change. The hordes of tourists and longer-stay visitors scurry about not even leaving scratch-marks. It is, par excellence, a *setting,* of enormous dramatic beauty. But all it gives off is a bitter sparkle.

Our introduction to this strange place was not auspicious. Used as we were to moving house, the fact of having to adapt to another dwelling was not in itself troublesome, but the flat that my mother had found for us was horrible—small, dingy and cramped. A flat which told of life lived at the meanest level of respectability, where the squalor of real want has been replaced by the ugliest and barest of material possessions. Hideous furniture—a settee and chairs covered in soot-and-dust coloured velveteen, beds with lean hair-filled mattesses reposing on busting springs. Curtains that hung skimpily round the black-out blinds. Drab parchment light shades. Knives that grew rust patches if they were not dried immediately. A bath with discoloured patches where the enamel was wearing thin, as if a thousand bums had rubbed it bare. The whole suffused with the gloom of insufficient daylight creeping in from north-facing windows. At the back, where sunlight could enter, there was the view of the washing green, a dull enclosed rectangle which we never used. Instead we went, or were sent to the King's Park, not many minutes' walk away, to climb the Crags or Arthur's Seat.

Despite its appalling dreariness, I was not at the time aware of any great sense of deprivation, for I still lived for much of the time in an inner world which retained a slightly feverish busyness, and there was in any case the outside world which was interesting enough to distract attention from our depressing living quarters. It took a long time for the novelty of riding on trams to wear off, besides which there was the thrill of two cinemas nearby, and a junk shop which we passed on the way to school where I spotted two beautiful fans, slightly broken but splendid with tarnished silver thread embroidery and ivory sticks. Resisting the fierce temptation to spend all my pocket money on roasted peanuts from the neighbourhood cafe, I saved up and acquired these treasures for, I think, 1/- and 2/6—a princely sum—respectively.

I had also been enrolled into regular ballet classes at a real ballet school, and from then on a bag containing dance tunic and ballet shoes became a kind of physical extension to my being, and my personal Edinburgh is, in fact, the tram routes which conveyed me to and from the ballet school to the various places where I lived.

But if I was relatively untroubled by home surroundings, my sister was not. She loathed the flat with a sort of horror-struck indignation, and being by then sixteen, opinionated and formidable to cross, she gave my mother a bad time. My mother was, I imagine, having a bad time in any case. A total stranger in the town, she had plumped for this extraordinary place, not because we were short of cash—my father sent an adequate allowance for our upkeep—but because, she told us afterwards, she was so riven with despair over the ravaged countries of Europe and their wandering, imprisoned, or destroyed peoples, that she felt it didn't matter where or how we lived, so long as we had roof over our heads. I can only think that such global hopelessness was a sign of deep depression and isolation, and, having had my own later experiences of being a single parent, there is no surprise in the fact of her depression. It is my guess that those first months in Edinburgh may have been near to breaking her.

How does a mother of young children, without any profession, make friends in a new place? Especially if she puts herself rather perversely in a limbo by living in a street where for social class reasons alone neighbourly relations are not likely to sprout easily? As a family we were already close-knit (too close for later comfort) and fairly self-sufficient; but even for the most devoted of parents the unbroken company of her children spells claustrophobia. She had only one outside interest, her connections with the Polish exiles, army and civilian, which she had made first in Moffat and extended to Edinburgh. By this time, she had taught herself to speak and read Polish with impressive fluency, and she helped out with a certain amount of editorial work and translation for various publications which they produced. This was probably stimulating, but it did nothing to put her in touch with greater Edinburgh.

Whatever stray intimations of my mother's anxieties and the tensions between her and my sister got through to me, home nonetheless remained a place of security, where the important people in my life were to be found. This, in spite of the fact that the ever-present irritation of sharing a room with my sister now reached a new level of animosity. I argued and quarrelled with her almost continuously, endlessly trying to assert myself and my ideas as of equal importance and merit as her own. I found it excruciatingly unjust that, simply because I was younger and smaller, what I said or thought carried less weight, and from then on for several years spent much energy in the frustrating and futile ambition of 'catching up' with Jill. One form this took was to imitate her slavishly in attending to personal appearance, a matter of very minor importance in the Moffat days. But if Jill were going to spend hours gazing at herself in the mirror, and making minute adjustments to her hair, so was I. Since there was only one dressing-table and one mirror in the room, this was a major source of squabbles, and indeed I feel for her, robbed of privacy to indulge a taste for self-contemplation more natural for a sixteen-year-old than an eleven-year-old.

From her I caught the hair neurosis. I should explain that at that time we both had long hair, worn in plaits. My mother had looked after our hair for years, and with my sister it had become a ritualised battle-ground. My mother's efforts were invariably wrong, too tight, or too loose, or the parting was squint, or the ribbons slack. Why she didn't hand over this unrewarding task at the first possible opportunity I don't know. Belatedly, Jill took over her own coiffure, and not so long after so did I—a great step towards adulthood and vanity. For by now gazing at myself in the mirror was becoming more pleasant. My bulging cheeks and double chin were fining down and something reasonably pretty was emerging. But I think that our shared obsession with mirrors was not only inturned vanity. I think we were more than a little unnerved by this curious watchful town where people in trams and shops appeared to be sizing one up by a secret system of weights and measures, and fled to establish ourselves in at least one pair of eyes—our own.

I wore my hair long until I was sixteen. It was then considered an asset for a dancer to have some length of hair. 'Ballerina style,' insisted upon for the classics, consisted of the hair drawn down from a centre parting over the ears and folded into a flat bun on the nape of the neck. My hair was always over-long to make this a very secure structure, and I wish to goodness I'd got rid of those plaits far sooner, for I had a tendency to hold my head too stiffly, and I don't think worrying about falling hair helped.

But once my long hair earned me a compliment which I treasured. It was not long after I had become a full-time dance student, which I did at fourteen. We were giving a public performance of some importance, dances from the *Sleeping Beauty* to illustrate a lecture given by Arnold Haskell, then, as for many years, holding sway as *the* pundit on ballet, and for a short exciting time deeply interested in Marjorie Middleton's ballet school and the students she was training up. 'He came into our dressing-room,' I recorded in the diary which I kept during my student years. 'I was standing brushing my hair with my tutu and tights and everything already on, and he said: "You look just like Giselle with a tutu on and your long hair. You keep that hair and you'll dance Giselle".'

Oh, great man, did you have any idea what happens to chance playful remarks like that? How they are kept like a talisman, an omen for the future, gilded with significance beyond your imagining? How in the search for signs of immortality these small portents are treasured by aspiring little girls? I never came within leagues of dancing 'Giselle', but at the time it seemed, like all coveted marks of approval, a tiny signpost assuring me I was taking steps along the road to glory.

School and Other Things

'You're a snobbery, snobbery, snobbery!' chanted an odious fat girl with short stumpy pigtails and squashed-back pug's nose. In my introduction to the venerable Edinburgh girls' school which consolidated what I have of early formal education this creature detached herself from the swarms of navy blue tunics and white blouses to declare her adenoidal judgment on me. It was not an attack that did much damage, for it hit on a fairly solid armour of resistance. I was not a snob, in spite of my expression of defensive superiority. At Moffat Academy no-one had called me a snob; it took petit-bourgeois Edinburgh to declare me one.

'Your hand-writing needs a lot of attention' said my form mistress bending with distaste over my copy-book. Gradually it got moulded from a spidery wandering longhand into the approved square 'print' which the school imposed on its pupils. That, however, took time. My rather poor control of pencil, pen or sewing needle was in fact about the most anxiety-provoking aspect of fitting myself into a new school, which suggests that the process was not too painful. By this time, after all, we were fairly used to changing schools.

My mother reminds me that when I first went to this institution, several hundreds strong, but a flea-bite compared to the giant comprehensives to be found today, I said I liked the orderliness of it all. It is an irritating reminder, for it goes against the ideas of a later self which abominates unnecessary regimentation. We were, typically, regimented. Long lines of navy-blue and maroon girls wound their way in orderly fashion up and down the complicated routes of main stairs, central gallery, side stairs and circumnavigating corridors, called to order at intervals by the lone figure of a prefect captaining her territorial section with curt commands: 'No talking on the stairs! Keep in single file.'

These big girls, privileged to wear skirts instead of tunics, and sporting the silver badge of office, were in our eyes half way to being staff members, which in fact they probably were. For the recruitment of old girls into the staff was a well-worn cycle and ensured that the school rolled on from generation to generation safeguarding the solid virtues of academic excellence, civic service to others and a totally unquestioning acceptance that life was an even progress from one well-defined role to the next. You can expect to find ex-pupils being dutiful wives and mothers or career women in the traditional women's professions—nursing, teaching and secretarial work, while the glory is gained from success in medicine, university lecturing, the civil service. My impression—and it is only that, for I left school too young to know for certain the varieties of exit into the real world—is that deviants became drop-outs rather than successes in any exotic way. It was a school which both educationally and socially taught with pernickety thoroughness the skills of categorising—an uncomfortable sort of place in which to be different.

Yet on the whole I managed to have the best of both worlds. I was different, but not outlandishly so. I thought it was because of my absorption in dancing, which since coming to Edinburgh had taken over most of my out-of-school hours. In fact, it was as much because my family had lived abroad, had moved, and had, compared with the matching sameness of the lives of most of the girls there, lived a roving life. With the sure recognition of common bonds, my friends in the first year were all girls who were not Edinburgh born and bred. One had a father in India, and I immediately endowed her and her family with a whole set of similarities to ourselves, a mistake rather drastically revealed by an encounter with her mother which occurred over one of those momentous theatrical occasions, a 'concert' which four of us had staged for the entertainment of parents and friends.

We were always planning concerts. But this one actually

23

happened, a real live performance of singing and dancing and 'recitations', and one daring semi-improvised play which we trusted ourselves to carry through without the bother of rigid scripting. It was nearly a disaster, for somewhere half way through it went off the rails, and the tale of eastern abduction and adventure showed every sign of lasting as long as *The Arabian Nights*, to the growing unease of our fidgetting parent audience. Somehow we managed to haul it back to its original conclusion, and there was a relieved storm of applause. The concert was voted a success, and we handed over an appreciable sum of money for the Charities Fund at school, where we were always being exhorted to do our bit for causes of our own choosing.

But in the midst of that triumph I was chewing away at a large lump of resentment, smarting with defeat over an issue which had blown up on the very eve of the performance. Mrs Silver, the mother of my friend Alison whose father was, like mine, in India, asked in her jolly, bouncy fashion what charity we were collecting for? She was a strong-featured dark-haired woman with sharp black eyes which slightly marred the general effect of jovial good-nature. 'The Indian Famine Relief' I said proudly. It had been my idea, partly inspired by concern about the appalling famine which had hit my old home country (as I still thought of it), and partly by a wish to break more exotic ground than the RSPCA, the Red Cross or Dr Barnardo's Homes.

Geniality disappeared in a flash. Mrs Silver whipped round. '*What* did you say?' I had no time to answer. 'You do that,' she went on passionately, 'and I won't put a penny piece in your collection. Not a halfpenny.' As a sneering afterthought she added: 'I'll put in a button if I have one!' I was winded with amazement. 'Why don't you want to give to the Famine Relief?' I managed to ask. She ranted on: 'Let them starve! Why should *I* give my money for a lot of lazy blacks? My son's a prisoner of war—you should be collecting for the Red Cross. In any case they're as rich as nabobs.' 'But it's food they need,' I protested, fatally opening the way for her triumphant retort: 'Then collecting money's not much use, is it?' Before I could work out

24

how British money could become food for Indians she had swept on, still high with anger: 'You make that collection for the Red Cross. I'll give plenty to that. But don't ask me to give money for that scum!'

I went home cramming the lid down on tears that overboiled hot and angry once I was safely inside the door. It was a disaster. The collection was all-important, the touchstone of success or failure. If a major contributor withheld we were in trouble; and Mrs Silver, unappeased, might wreck the whole occasion. I was fearfully upset, due in part to the savaging I'd received, and in part to utter confusion as to why she was so insanely angry.

My mother tried to calm me down, all sympathy, but she did not then offer any theories. I'm sorry the possibility of defiance was never raised. My mother took the diplomatic viewpoint that we'd better give in and collect for the Red Cross. I still wish I'd defied Mrs Silver and ridden out the unpleasantness of her wrath at the concert. I was furious at the blackmail that she'd used on us; but my best performance of the occasion was to make the announcement, as chief organiser and spokesman, that the collection now to be taken was in aid of the Red Cross and we hoped everyone would give generously to this worthy cause. From my stance out front I saw Mrs Silver nodding and smiling in a satisfied I-told-you-so way.

By degrees, some light was shed on her mysterious anger.

I picked up from some slightly evasive remarks by my mother that there might well be a touch of colour in the Silver family, which to her at least made complete sense of the outburst I'd provoked. Anglo-Indians had no fond feelings for the race they were determined to disown. Also, as my friendship with Alison progressed, I came to realise that Mrs Silver was not at all anxious to be rejoined to her absent husband. The Silver household was, in fact, intriguingly different from family life as I'd known it. Alison had two adult sisters from whom she was rapidly learning a lot of fascinating worldly knowledge, mainly about men. One sister was already in the throes of ending her first marriage. Another was a luscious, plump, dark-eyed young woman who

25

even to my puritanically childish ideas suggested nothing but fruity sexuality.

Under such tutelage, it's not surprising that Alison was well in the van of my class-mates in starting the love game. She was soon exchanging notes with a tall red-haired boy, son of one of the direst of Presbyterian families, using his limp holy-willy sister as go-between, and myself as favoured confidante. Or so I believed, but, who knows, she may have had favoured confidantes sprinkled all over the place. For purposes of symmetry I was paired up with a friend of her swain, an unattractive youth with bunched teeth and shorts revealing unmuscular legs, and since I was still at the stage of wearing knee-length socks and the shortest of gym-tunics with a long expanse of chilled thigh exposed, I can't think we made a very exciting couple, nor that I had any great value in the emotional exchange-and-mart which Alison was so speedily entering.

It was probably then that we drifted apart and I became close friends with Pat, a troubled, unhappy, talented girl who seemed to set my tastes for a lifetime in the direction of complex and conflicted people—who are, often, intelligent and gifted beyond the ordinary, but do not make for a smooth passage in relationships.

Before that, however, I went through a period of ostracism at school which fortunately started not long before the end of the summer term, so that by the end of the succeeding long summer vacation its cause had faded in my class-mates' memories. Schoolgirl ethics are strong and lasting, and I still don't enjoy admitting to the fact that I cheated in an exam, particularly as I had no need to cheat. The subject was French in which I was a year behind the others, having only started to learn when I came to this school. However, I had picked it up rapidly and was hoping urgently to get into the top stream when we moved to senior school. I was racing happily through the exam paper when to my disgust I ran into a vocabulary question which floored me. The temptation to flip open my grammar surreptitiously (in primary school there was no formal banishing of text books from exams) came, not from a desperate situation of tipping the balance towards a pass, but from sheer pique at not getting that 100 per cent mark I was so near to achieving. I looked up the phrase, completed the exam, and scored my bull's-eye as the results eventually confirmed. But of course I'd been spotted—not by my teacher but by a class-mate, and a buzz got around that had girls who were friendly with me coming up with troubled faces and tales of horrible rumours. They were clearly waiting and hoping for enough righteous indignation on my part to put their minds at ease, but not surprisingly my performance was half-hearted. I ought to have a painful memory of slinking around, pariah-like for the rest of term, but the defence-mechanism eraser seems to have worked effectively in this instance. I only know that I never owned up to this sin at home, and that by the next term it was stale stuff, ancient history, and I had more or less a clean start. In any case, we had been reshuffled and my most indignant accusers were now divided from me by that incredibly solid barrier, the academic streaming system.

Thus ended my first year in Edinburgh during which, rather to my surprise, it seems that school and schoolfellows have purloined most of the memory space, leaving dancing and music apparently in the background. Yet it was during that year that I came under teachers in both subjects who played a major formative part in my adolescence, if not my life. It is probably unfair to contrast the inspirational effect of one with the other. In music, I never went deep enough as a participant to develop the lasting closeness of pupil and master who go through the fire and flood of the former's development together. Thus Hans Gal remains one of the few people in my life who shine out as revealing something of the enormous emotional power and breadth of an art. He was and is a fine musician, and a man of high intellect, and I do not believe that my deep respect and gratitude is only because I took music lightly enough for it to remain at the level of pleasure with few ordeals. It was he who gave me music as it has always been since that time, the supreme joy without which I would certainly perish. And I am glad, in

27

fact, that my broken love affair with an art was with ballet rather than music. It would be intolerable to feel the inadequacies of commitment and sense of shoddy failure with regard to music that I eventually felt towards dancing.

However, at eleven I was a long way from any such feelings. Marjorie Middleton, who taught me from that age till I was sixteen ran a large ballet school. She was also a large lady with a certain kind of four-square dignity which was impressive, and from my very first private lesson with her I knew we meant business in a way that had never happened with earlier teachers. She taught me well and patiently and until I became a student I had absolutely no inkling of the more unrestrained aspects of her leadership, that as well as being the respected captain of the ship she could also be a tyrannical overseer. But of that I shall write later. At this point I only want to say that she never was, despite her capability, inspirational in the peculiar sense that I mean, which is to possess the quality that makes the learning of a subject illumine not only itself but life and the world as well. I am sure this should happen in any kind of intensive learning. Whatever the subject, the process of learning is also a process of discovering about being in the world. One goes deeper and wider than simply the matter in hand.

My main grouse against ballet is that it never did that, and in this respect I think a fairly sharp distinction has to be made between traditional ballet and modern dance. Modern dancers who work with gifted teachers and choreographers talk of this enriching process, to do with a life-view and a philosophy coming through the creative work in which they are involved. Ballet, in my admittedly limited experience, was narrowly concerned with nothing but itself. I have never understood what a ballet dancer's life view is, nor what they discover about themselves as people except their capacities to endure and drive themselves and swallow their panic.

As a personality, ballet was an unfortunate choice for me to have made. I already had enough troublesome tendencies to get locked away in a remote narcissistic world of my own, enough problems with making contact with 'reality'. But in opposition to that I also had a lot of healthy curiosity, about other people and other cultures, and an appetite for mental stimulation which, again, the world of ballet left totally unsatisfied. I was eventually to reach screaming point at its appalling restrictive narrowness.

While I remained at school however I managed to keep up a range of other activities. Sporty I never was by inclination and by the age of twelve or thirteen it was banned by Marjorie in case I got my knees whacked by a hockey stick or strained my back wielding a tennis racquet. While I can appreciate that some of these safeguards were necessary, I suspect that the embargo on sport was also part of the indoctrination of single-mindedness. Sport aside, I took part in various extra-curricular pursuits—school plays, singing, even Girl Guides for a little while, and in collaboration with my friend Pat, the private venture of publishing a magazine. For I was also a writing enthusiast and had already started, but never finished, a novel about—guess what?—a girl studying ballet.

The magazine, however, was totally unconnected with art; it was intended as a satire (though not a very subtle one) on various down-market women's magazines. Blushing, I have to confess that the *People's Friend* was a frequent source-book of ideas. We even cut out the illustrations and invented our own stories round them. The magazine ran to three laboriously prepared copies of each termly number. And we sweated against our dead-line as copiously as any professional editors. Pat could type after a fashion and she also looked after the graphics. The most dreaded chore was producing further instalments, in collaboration, of the serial story we'd been foolish enough to start. Our main let-out was the three blank pages left for the agony column, by far the most popular section of the publication. Readers queued up to subscribe for it mainly for the fun of inventing searing problems which were pencilled in and signed 'Heartbroken' or 'Ready to die' or 'Puzzled', and which we were challenged to remedy in the next issue.

I don't remember how long we kept up this *tour de force,* but we certainly collected impressive enough amounts—for charity, of course—to rouse the curiosity of the staff. It was always a horror looming over us that a member of staff would actually read it, for it was at a level of private silliness that should never be exposed to adult eyes. I wish I'd remembered, once I became a parent, the right of children to be totally and completely corny. It was in fact confiscated once during a singing class as it was being passed surreptitiously along to the next subscriber, and the singing-master, a small disenchanted gnome of sarcasm who quite openly loathed schoolgirls and girls' schools, flicked over its grimed pages and treated us to a selection of the purplest and silliest pieces of dialogue. ' "Oh, don't leave me", she exclaimed passionately. Dear me, whatever next? "His handsome head was bent over her parted lips." Is this the only result of exposure to Milton and Shakespeare? Who is responsible for this rubbish?' Crimson in the face, Pat and I raised our hands. He looked surprised when he saw that I was co-author—perhaps he thought I was too intellectually inclined for such follies and handed back our poor magazine as though it were something slightly insanitary. Thereafter I changed my opinion of Mr Bowman who till then I had pitied for his swivelling wall eye, his ghastly position as one of four masters in an otherwise all-female establishment, and the fact that he was only five foot two.

In spite of magazine love-stories, both the ones I read and those we concocted, I took a very haughty line about girls whose only interest in life was boys. There seemed, in my observation, to be some correlation between poor academic performance and a tendency to spend the entire lunch-hour huddled in the cloakrooms, trying out hairstyles and gossiping about—well, if not sex, then the other sex. Family attitudes, which covered a basic embarrassment on the subject of sexual attraction under a pose of superior dismissal, was reinforced by the school, which channelled its pupils by an efficient sluicing system into a dire partition between the bright and the not-so-bright. The latter were left relatively free to become either sporty or sexy.

My immunity from the temptation of girlish gossip was

accentuated by the fact that I was not only younger than my class-mates but years behind in physical development. Also I genuinely did enjoy stretching my mind, as long as it entailed no sustained effort, and found the interminable talk about boys flat and uninspiring. There was still another factor. What I was already after, knew in my heart of hearts was the only thing worth going for, was passion. Not for me the mediocrity of these little tickles of attraction which were fed into the game of, 'And he said to me and I said to him', while the listening group waited for an opening to interrupt and take a turn as chief raconteur. I was prepared to wait.

The Man of Reason

In 1944, when I was twelve, my father reappeared in my life on his first leave from India. He arrived one evening after dark. There must have been some kind of build up to the event, but I can remember only the actual encounter. More accurately, I can only remember the awful sense of disappointment when the great moment arrived—the fearful chill, the constraint, the unease, whereas I'd anticipated an instant ecstatic reunion and an immediate sense of fatherhood. The man himself was a disappointment, a remote stranger, impenetrably reserved. But the fact was, we *were* total strangers, all of us children. It was seven years since I'd last seen him, and nine since my brother and sister had left him in India. What little I remembered of him was still surrounded by an aura of Indian sunshine, and the official dignity of having a crowd of uniformed messengers sitting permanently around on the verandah outside his office ready to spring on bicycles and do his bidding.

The circumstances of our reunion were far from propitious. My father, shrivelled and chilled by a dark Scottish autumn, was horrified to find us living where we were. The contrast between his semi-aristocratic life-style in India, which war-time and the unsettled political state of the country had not markedly changed, and the dismal pokiness of our flat produced a sense of culture shock. My mother, whom he had last seen presiding over dinner tables and carrying out similarly gracious hostess duties, now scrubbed her own floors. He was strained and tired, and the resumption of their relationship was not easy. They had parted when she was a relatively young and untried woman. Several years of single-parenthood had made deep changes in the direction of independence.

To make up for my first disenchantment I soon fell in love with my father. His first reserve thawed out, and the humour and sweetness which it so formidably hid was revealed. I thought he was wonderful. I thought he was the fountainhead of all authority and knowledge which, because he was a scholarly and keenly intelligent man, was not difficult for him to sustain. I suspect, too, that I warmed to the role of cheering him up, and that after that first forbidding encounter even his sombreness appealed to me. He only stayed long enough on that first leave to move us into a different flat, not wonderful but vastly improved, before he had to return for his final stint in India.

The new flat, set back by a long glass-roofed corridor from a busy cheerful street of shops and small businesses, was sunny and roomy enough for my sister and myself at last to have a room each and end the infernal duet of bickering and sniping which had accompanied the last few years. Thereafter we could more or less do what we wanted without getting in each others' hair, which, considering the inordinate amount of time we both used to spend over our coiffures, is an apt enough metaphor.

Whether it was my father's influence, which, being the kind of man he was, could only be in the direction of great seriousness, or whether it was simply that I was growing up, I don't know. But almost overnight, after the move, I set new standards for myself. About things that I'd been wildly careless over, I suddenly became obsessionally neat, sewing, for example. Up till then it had been a matter of hasty tacking stitches cobbling a few bits of material together to make garments for the dressing-up box, while at school my hemming round the edge of outsize bloomers or sack-like nightdresses caused the sewing mistress to recoil with a kind of fastidious distaste. Now, I aspired to perfection, invisible regular stitching.

My handwriting also capitulated and started to regularise into the boxy neatness of the 'print' which the school had been struggling for the best part of two years to impose on me. And,

inspired at least in part by this novel control over my pen, I
started to keep a personal diary, MY JOURNAL, as I entitled it.
It turned out to be a long-lasting activity, lapsing sometimes for
years, but always sooner or later resumed in one form or another.
Intermittently it still flourishes, something I turn to when I get an
attack of that strange malaise which afflicts people who keep
journals which are other than simply documentary, a sense of
being out of touch with one's own existence. But in the
beginning it served no such introspective need, it was simply a
whim.

The most significant change was in my attitude towards ballet.
From then on I knew that I was engaged in a long task of
reshaping myself in accordance with its dictates. It was no longer
simply a question of going and doing one's best at class and
dancing nicely. There were physical shortcomings to be
corrected, one's body to be made over and trained in quite specific
ways. I had not, of course, worked all this out for myself. My
teacher told me the kinds of things I must practice, and practice I
did—fanatically. In the new and comparatively spacious flat there
was room to work in front of a mirror in the hall, and evening
after evening I went through a routine of exercises to lower my
over-square shoulders, to strengthen my point-work, to loosen
the ligaments in my legs, to increase the height and upward curve
of my arabesque. In order to do so, I drew on a source of energy
which till then I didn't know I possessed, but without which no
dancer can hope to stay the pace. That is a kind of masochism
which notches up the pain and the bruised and skinned toes as
valuable evidence of dedication, that takes positive satisfaction
from the aches of stretched tendons, the groans of overworked
muscles and the all-out fatigue at the end of a hard class.

As in any activity which requires the development of the body
well beyond its everyday level of functioning, it is essential to
have that capacity to push oneself relentlessly, in the face of all
temptations to slide away from the final effort. But there is such a
thing as pushing oneself too eagerly and too impatiently with the
possibility of doing quite serious damage. I had been given an

exercise to help develop those ideal curved high arches in the feet, which was to sit with the feet tucked under a piece of furniture with a small space between its base and the floor—certain chests of drawers were ideal. Trying to straighten the knees in this position exerted a severe pull on the insteps. In my new fanaticism, I used to sit and pull away until my big toe joints were red and sore with the pressure, and my Achilles's tendons aching with being bunched under. As with this, so with other exercises. I strained and forced my feet and back, on the principle that if an exercise was going to develop suppleness, then the more often I did it, the quicker I would become supple. And certainly I was soon able to extend my legs acrobatically in all directions; but, unknown, I was piling up trouble for the future. If I were teaching young dancers I would watch like a hawk for signs of this over-punitive haste in their development.

Because it now seems to me that a child's quality of enjoyment is about the most precious thing we ever experience—either as children or adults—I can't think of that period in the way that I experienced it. I remember quite clearly enough to know that as I lived it, the excitement of aspiring, of aiming high, of getting some tentative mastery over new skills, the bouts of rhapsodical joy which dancing brought, quite drowned out the anxiety which was the inevitable counter-theme. The future was open, time was fluid, washing out bad moments as easily as sun after a storm. Yet I also know that it was the end of a particular inconsequential exhilaration—the point which comes inevitably where a naive relationship of wellbeing with the world is broken—if one has been lucky enough to have that as a child. Thereafter energy came from changed sources, motivations which are familiar enough. I wanted to please people, to do well. I was prepared to strive and to worry. Things started to matter with a kind of burning importance. Life, in spite of its teeming interest, was no longer a set of pathways along which to chase capricious fantasies. It became serious at the core, with some vague apprehension of root conflict involved, prices to pay.

Some of this I imagine I picked up from my father's presence and the continuing tensions between him and my mother. It must have been a sombre time for him, aged fifty-five, tired and in poor health, faced with the necessity of starting again. Like many of his colleagues he had difficulty in getting a job, not helped in his case by being awarded a knighthood. People are almost invariably reluctant to employ an overqualified person; with 'Sir' tacked onto one's name the doors close even faster. Eventually he got into the home Civil Service; but before that there was a period of many months of uncertainty and, I suspect, deep depression.

I've already described him as a man of extreme reserve. It was his defence against something he held in real dread, the exposure of personal feelings. It added to the special nature of our relationship that I felt confident I had access to this concealed part of him, that I knew, if no one else did, about the humour and playfulness and tenderness which was hidden behind the mask of steady reason. Over the years I discovered with pain that to put oneself in the role of the expressive agent, if I can put it that way, for people who bury their emotions deep is a losing role. It is also an arrogant one, as is any attempt to demonstrate to people that they are other than they think they are. My father lived his life consistent with the belief that reason rules over feeling, and he did not die a pathetic and unfulfilled man. If I believe that there was a whole side of him, the sensual, artistically gifted side, that hardly saw the light of day, that was his choice. Yet I feel like protesting—still. Because as a child one is not mistaken about the quality of undeclared emotions. And his rigorous self-suppression was something too heavy to be ignored by anyone close to him. If I had not had the seeds of the same conflict between an over-orderly intellectual schema and powerful but chaotic emotional energies, he would not have affected me so strongly. If I hadn't loved him so very much, I wouldn't have wanted to solve his problems, to comfort him, which is how I felt about him when I was a child.

I think of him now as a sort of classical temple, estimably expressing solid elegant order, but with no space in the formal excellence of the design for the unexpected, the absurd, for sheer dotty fun, for flights of fantasy or inspiration. He had a fine, intuitive intelligence, for all that, but he exercised it principally in the form of criticism. To have to show something to my father, whether it was a new dress, a new hairstyle, a piece of work or a performance, meant steeling oneself to face one of the most devastating critical faculties I've ever encountered. It was not a question of unkindness, simply that he saw no merit in tempering his judgments, or in interrupting the process of 'pure criticism'. Thus, in the gentlest of ways, and without being aware of it, he established a sort of reign of terror for me—terror of not living up to the standards of this most important of people in my life.

Certainly his homecoming changed the quality of our family life. It added a chilly refinement, opened up a world of aesthetic appreciation through his interest in art and architecture and literature, but damped down a lot of natural frivolity. The last months on our own without him, the flat was full of loud, uncultural noise. A cousin called up to the army had left us his gramophone and collection of records—Frank Sinatra, Carmen Miranda, the Mills Brothers, Hogey Carmichael and other popular vocalists of the times. We played them over and over, and I, still a compulsive exhibitionist, used to give impersonations of the singers in front of visitors, to the excrutiating embarrassment of my brother and sister, flouncing my way through Carmen Miranda's numbers with all the precocious sexiness of a Lena Zavaroni. Then it was banjo time. My brother bought one so I must have one too, and all one holidays we strummed duets at full volume until the craze was spent. Nothing like that happened after the reappearance of my father. He used to ask rather wistfully why I wouldn't do my impersonations in front of him? I would rather have died in the fiery furnace than expose my foolishness to him in that fashion, for he had a most unhappy knack of drying up spontaneity.

He was however intensely interested in my dancing, being something of a balletomane himself. He had seen Pavlova dance, he had seen Dhiaghilev's Ballets Russes, and once he had travelled to India on the same boat as the De Basil company and had spent most of the voyage watching them at class and rehearsal. There was no question of a reluctant conversion to my cause, though whether he foresaw when we first met up that I would want to train seriously, I don't know.

Certainly, I encountered no opposition from either parent, though I suspect my mother had to do some persuasive talking with my father when fundamental career decisions had to be made. Being allowed to do what one is yearning to do is in many ways excellent, and my parents were probably rarities in acting as they did, especially as I had enough academic ability to make university seem the inevitable outcome in the eyes of all my teachers. But no parent gets it exactly right. My mother's own investment in my dancing was intense and emotionally charged, a vicarious dream come true. As a child, she had been told she was ideally suited for ballet and this must have lingered on in her imagination; my dancing was her trip as well as mine.

Ballet mothers are a standard joke in the ballet world; fiercely involved in the fate of their young flowers, and ready to gouge out the eyes of unsympathetic teachers or ballet-masters, legend (and sometimes reality) has it that they sit in dressing-rooms like guardian dragons watching over the interests of the wonder-child. The sight of the genuine article in full battle-cry is as impressive as an Armada galleon firing a broadside—I have seen hardened administrators pale and quail before the onslaught. My mother was nothing like such cartoon figures, except in the degree of her absorption in my 'artistic dedication'. Being the exception in a sober-toned family which on both sides prided itself on the efficient use of its brain-power to achieve professional success, it was fatally easy for me to become a figure of high romance, in my own eyes and in hers. Notions of almost saint-like specialness, someone set apart by the call to artistry and other-worldiness, abounded in our shared fantasies. It is a dangerous air to breathe. If ever there is a need to keep extra cool and well-grounded in commonsense, it is in the business of 'managing' the training of someone entering one of the artistic professions. It is brutally tough from start to finish, and wonder-children do not survive long.

There is another important point—the let-out clause. Should a decision taken at the age of fourteen, or even earlier, be like a marriage vow? Recently I talked to the head of a specialist music school, and was relieved to hear her stress the importance of children being given the opportunity to decide against a career in music, even after several years of intensive training. It is a matter of such importance that, as she quite rightly said, there should be an enforced pause for a rethink, time and opportunity to air doubts, remake the decision one way or another, rather than get swept on by the force of one's own and other people's investments in the situation.

Until I was sixteen I had hardly a moment's doubt that I wanted to be a dancer. 'I don't think you realise how difficult it would have been to stop you' my mother once said. About the first few years she is absolutely right. When, however, I started to have some regrets about what I was missing out on, it was probably time for some careful thought. But I shovelled my doubts out of sight, and kept on, partly because of a still existing passion for dancing, partly because of the threat of an almost total loss of identity. By that time, too, I knew uneasily that there were other people's emotions strongly involved.

By the time I was fourteen it was clear that normal schooling and dancing could no longer co-exist. I was attending something like five classes a week, plus long Sunday afternoons at the Ballet Club, founded by Marjorie Middleton presumably in emulation of Marie Rambert's famous pioneer group at the Mercury Theatre. In the weeks before performances, which the Ballet Club gave every few months, there were late evening rehearsals several times a week. I think it was from then on that I was menaced by the thing I hold most resentfully against my experiences as a dancer—desperate fatigue, intermittent to begin with, becoming chronic in time. Dancers require the stamina of shire horses, which I never possessed.

To the dismay and consternation of my schoolteachers, my parents agreed that I should leave school and become a full-time student at Marjorie Middleton's ballet school. It was considered bizarre, a frightful waste of potential. But I was overjoyed, not because of leaving school which I liked well enough, but because this was the first real step towards becoming a professional dancer. What I didn't realise, as I departed in a modest blaze of glory, with a couple of prizes, a sprightly performance in an end of term play, and a fair measue of popularity, was that it was also putting on me a path so different that I would never really link up with 'normal' adolescent life again. Thereafter I was an outsider, and have remained one ever since.

The Dance Studio

When I first joined Marjorie's school as an eleven-year-old her studio was a light airy room perched high above the shops in Princes Street. Something reasonably civilised in the way of a changing room flanked it on one side, permanently seething with little girls dragging their white regulation tunics and pink or black leather ballet shoes out of cases, and usually chaperoned by hatted and fur-jacketed mothers. However, the year I became a student the school had moved to premises more spacious but grimed for all time with dirt and decay. I think it must have been at one time a warehouse or store. Like every ballet studio I have ever worked in, this place was cold and cheerless. Cold water running into an old-fashioned square china sink was the only washing facility, and it doubled up as the place where coffee and teacups were washed, and paint brushes soaked off when costumes and scenery were being painted. One long room with practise barres stretched over the area covered at ground level by Thin's bookshop and several smaller shops—we were one floor up. There was a second room where we changed and which, as function demanded, was also used as a dumping ground for props and costumes. At lunch-break, if we didn't go out to a nearby milk-bar, we huddled round an ancient and inadequate gas fire. And, like every other studio, the thick smell of sweat-rotted garments pervaded the air.

For the next two years I spent most of my waking existence in this place. Morning class was from eleven till one o'clock, afternoon classes from two till four. Private lessons were squeezed into the lunch hour, or before morning class. Once a week we had to stay on to teach the children's classes which started at four in the afternoon. And more often than not there were evening rehearsals for performances as well as a once-weekly adagio class, when pas-de-deux work was practised and one prayed for a partner with strong arms and a good sense of timing.

Attendance at the Sunday afternoon Ballet Club rehearsals was compulsory, though to my huge resentment it often meant sitting for hours huddled up in woollies against the cold, doing nothing but watch others rehearse. 'I hate these long, long rehearsals,' I wrote in my journal soon after I'd joined the ranks as a very junior student. 'The Ballet Club seems to get right into my system, the dust, the dirt, the disorder, everything. If I ever made a lot of money I'd have a studio built, a model studio, with showers, pleasant dressing-rooms, everything.'

My first reaction to my new environment was, in fact, one of dismaying negativity. The great step had been taken, but it was no enchanted existence I had entered, and for the first few months I was critical and unfriendly at the studio, and bad-tempered and complaining at home to the point that my mother, exasperated, started to doubt the wisdom of having taken me away from school.

Going to the dance studio after orthodox schooling was an experience of considerable culture-shock. I missed my schoolfriends acutely and unexpectedly. I also missed the atmosphere of 'book-learning' and mental activity. At school we may have skived homework and developed a rota system for producing master-copies of written exercises. We may have had our cruel rating system whereby certain staff members were fair game for any kind of sly abuse. But basically we accepted the idea of schooling and academic learning (at least in patches) and did not feel the need to hide our interest in certain subjects, any more than we needed to hide our boredom with others.

At the studio I found myself among girls at the level of shop-girl literacy. If I was not a snob when I first went to my Edinburgh school, I certainly was by the time I left—a mental snob. It was not social background that bothered me, it was what I saw as dreary empty-headedness, intellectual apathy and an incuriosity about facts, ideas, or any experiences outside the four walls of the studio, that drove me demented. Passionately I used to complain: 'Nobody wants to talk about anything here.' I was a great enthusiast for talk, good argumentative discussion. A certain scornful puritan superiority, a horribly exaggerated seriousness about self-improvement made me savagely critical of the amiable chattering crowd of girls who were my fellow students. It wore off in time and I made my friends (though none very close) and changed them and got caught up in studio gossip and the mini-politics of shallow love affairs. But for those first months I was not happy, and since I was also incapable of concealing my reactions to others, I was hardly a popular figure.

Another shock to the system came from the new persona of Marjorie Middleton, whom till then I had experienced as a gracious and kindly figure presiding over children's classes, or being carefully attentive at private lessons. Now she emerged as a tough tyrant, and about the only group feeling I immediately tuned into was a universal grousing resentment against her. For some time my own relationship to her was quite over-written by the set script attaching to our respective roles. As a junior newcomer I was at the bottom of the rigid hierarchy of the ballet-class, subdivided by the rungs of the Royal Academy of Dancing examination system. It seemed to be accepted, if resented, that she had the right or the licence to shout and bully, to create scapegoats and favourites, and I reacted violently against this, although I was not personally at the receiving end of her volleys of expressive abuse. But I felt betrayed, and rather horror-struck at the emergence of this unvarnished power-wielder. I am painting an exaggerated picture, or rather, a one-sided picture in order to point up the comical contrast with my previous idealisations. To my little-girl self 'Miss Middleton' had been just marvellous, wise, kind, patient, dignified and super-human. Now I was seeing her in the raw. The fantasy, self-projected, was bound to be shattered. Furthermore, there was the little matter of jealousy. I no longer had a privileged place in the sun. Part of my first term anger was to find myself one of the ruck of small-fry relegated to the back of the class. As I worked my way forwards, with time and the passing of those all-important examinations, my feelings towards her inevitably shifted back to the semi-adoration of the special pupil.

Nevertheless, the sway she had over our lives always rankled. Perhaps some element of tyranny is almost inevitable in teaching ballet. I can only recollect two or three teachers in my whole experience in Edinburgh, London and Paris who were *not* full-blown tyrants. Perhaps, given that part of the task is to goad or exhort people to total exertion hour after hour, the temptation to resort to galley-slave techniques (omitting actual flagellation) is irresistible. What I picked up with anger was the *licence* that this situation gave to the teacher, and Marjorie took full and in my view, unfair, advantage of this.

There was much more to her than mere tyranny, however. I've described her elsewhere as 'ogre, fairy godmother, taskmaster and generous good sport' and she was all those things, as well as a source of leaderly energy which we all drew on. A woman with a broad sense of humour, she was a heavyweight, both physically and in terms of personality, with the kind of stamina that never lets up, and pushes on through one seven-day week after another, which nearing performance time meant something like an eighteen-hour day.

In other words, Marjorie was formidable; she ground on like a tank through disaffection in the ranks and disappointed hopes about the ballet company she had wanted to start. Sulk and grumble as we did about her relentless methods, we all looked to her and her alone to supply the drive needed to pass our exams and perform on stage.

In the last weeks before a show we would all be drafted in to help sew or paint costumes, and her flat in central Edinburgh, which she shared with her two children and an indeterminate number of dogs and visitors, became the centre of operations. Compared to the rather bleak orderliness of my own home (only I didn't experience it as such at the time, thinking that the boxy

Victorian house my father had bought spelt domestic perfection) the jumblesale confusion of Marjorie's residence was startling. She herself was often to be found, as though holding some travesty of a *grande levée,* in the middle of a large double bed surrounded by dogs, organdie frills, feathers, ribbon, paper, beads—anything and everything that could be disgorged from those bulging hoards of treasure and junk which seemed to fill every chest and cupboard. From this central position she organised us into making flowers and ornaments for head-dresses and bodices, or machining miles and miles of tarlatan into ballet skirts on her treadle sewing machine. At other times our wretched mothers were forced into doing their bit, as cowed by Marjorie's long-distance commands to cut out the bodice of a tu-tu, or create a Greek nymph's costume with the scantiest of guidance, as we were. It was undoubtedly the most nightmarish part of the ballet experience for my own mother, who loathed dressmaking and collapsed with a sense of total inadequacy under these unclear but forceful commands, but nevertheless nobly produced the goods.

Marjorie must have been in her early forties when I first became a student. I know very little about her previous life. There were one or two studio photos of her as a dancer, but they showed that already as a young woman she had the squareness of build which in later years turned to overweight of the kind that refuses to be constrained. Like most ballet teachers she totally neglected her appearance except when she was due to appear as public representative of her ballet school. Then, dramatically transformed, she would appear for all her size as a handsome, even distinguished, woman. Her unkempt greying hair, nicotine stained from the cigarette permanently grafted onto her upper lip, was miraculously subdued. Her amazing unspoilt complexion bloomed against a black frock. Her dazzling smile softened the masculine squareness of her face. She shone with charismatic warmth. But apart from these state occasions, usually at the end of a performance or when giving a lecture-demonstration, she simply let it all hang out. In that respect she reminded me of another forceful charming woman with a similarly chaotic attitude to everyday life, my aunt Nan, whose maxim was: 'Make an effort for parties, and for the rest it doesn't matter a damn.' They were both, I suppose, so supremely confident in their pesonal magnetism that little things like wrinkled laddered stockings, burst zips and collapsing footwear were unimportant. Marjorie's everyday gear was either a pair of elephantine slacks or a worn tartan skirt, enveloped for street wear in a large tartan cloak. Everything she wore looked as though it doubled up for nightwear. But, as I say, it takes a certain impressive largeness of personality to carry off what for smaller, more nervously inhibited mortals would be unthinkable.

There was undoubtedly more than a sniff of Bohemia in Marjorie's dwelling place and entourage. Yet, although in these early days when the Edinburgh Festival was in its infancy her Ballet Club in its modest and undeniably parochial way supplied a focus for the arts, the strongest quality that emanated from her was the unshakeable, earthbinding pragmatism of the native Scot. It is a heart-breaking quality. Once imbued with it, you may try and soar, you may rebel in all sorts of colourful and outrageous ways. You will never entirely break or lose it. It is a grounding quality, the essence of dogmatic commonsense which can be guaranteed to puncture all but the most powerful of artistic visions with a thrust of banality.

At the time I trained with Marjorie her teaching was good. She taught us carefully and thoroughly and instilled in us a sense of high standard, though she was not sufficiently alert to the possibilities of strain and over-forcing. As for her choreography, I don't think she had more than a moderate talent—but then many superlative teachers lack this gift. In retrospect, what I missed most was any contact with a distinctive aesthetic sense, and also any sense of her emotional involvement with ballet. I don't know what she felt about ballet, or dance. Perhaps it was because, teacher and students alike, we were almost all steeped in that atmosphere of dour dismissal of matters of feelings that I've referred to. It is remarkable that the only exceptions to this buttoned-lip attitude were two or three Jewish girls, for whom, apparently, being expressive did not hold the ungodly terrors of self-exposure which kept the majority bottled up behind a kind of prim priggish simper.

Marjorie insisted, quite rightly, that her younger students should continue with some modicum of schooling, so half a dozen of us studied school subjects for an hour and a half each morning before ballet class. Unfortunately, our tutor lived at the opposite side of town from the studio. Our mid-morning break was a fast trot down the road to catch a bus, which, if it appeared on time, meant that we just scraped into class for the first exercises, and if it did not, caused us to miss our *pliés.* My parents wanted me to take some kind of academic qualification (and thank God they did), so while the rest simply sat through lessons unconcerned I was preparing seven subjects for the now obsolete School Certificate. For this purpose I had an extra maths class one afternoon a week which entailed more dashing across town and often no time to go home before evening rehearsal. My tutor was a kindly lady and fed me cocoa and biscuits when I was looking particularly peaky. As well as this, there were music lessons with Hans Gal, too often under-practised, which I felt sad and bad about because I loved him and my music as well. Homework had somehow to be fitted into this schedule, and until I had sat and passed my School Certificate there was, bar Saturday afternoons and Sunday mornings, hardly a half-hour in the week I could call my own. I was not infrequently out from half past eight in the morning till after nine at night.

This used sometimes to produce a state of exhaustion bordering on hysteria. Always erratic in mood, I think some of the dramas were made shriller simply through being stretched too far. 'God! What an evening I've just passed through' I wrote with self-conscious melodrama in my diary, 'Tears, storms and passions—' And the cause? Nothing more dreadful than a harmony exercise which I couldn't do. On another occasion, my brother's taunt that he knew more about ballet than I did about cricket (his obsession at the time) grew from mild cat-fighting into

47

a full-scale row which required fatherly intervention before I foamed at the mouth with rage at such insolence. I must have been nearly intolerable to live with.

Although I fairly quickly fell into the way of studio life, and shared in the pre-exam traumas and the alternate fun and boredom of the performances we gave in and around Edinburgh, I remained an intermittent insurrectionary throughout the first year. Efforts at independence were hardly of the kind to threaten the status quo. A few of us tried to organise a hike over the Pentlands for one Sunday afternoon instead of attending the long, tedious Ballet Club rehearsal, but our acute tyrant got wind of it and deflated us with a particularly pointed reminder that *all* rehearsals must be attended by every member, after which we lost our nerve. But one day at class I made history, a solitary little rebellion whose impact on my classmates was quite the most staggering part of the whole experience.

Quite simply, I stopped the class. We had worked for two hours, as usual, hard and without let-up, and were standing panting and sweating and looking with doggy hopefulness, knowing we had only two or three minutes to go. Perhaps Marjorie, if she was merciful, would say 'Curtseys' straight away and dismiss us. Miss Middleton looked at her watch; her eyes flicked back to the waiting class. She paused fractionally—and set us another exercise. With a groan of dismay we started to mark it out, then to do it properly. She set us another, and another. By this time there was a subdued simmering of protest but still we obediently fell back into place and started to trace out the steps, until suddenly something snapped and I found myself saying clearly out loud, and without conscious volition: 'Miss Middleton, what time is this class supposed to end?' There was a dumbfounded breath-held silence. 'One o'clock, dear,' she said, admirably mild. 'Why? Surely it can't be that time yet?' With an elaborate stage gesture she consulted her watch. 'Dear me,' she murmured, 'I thought it was only half past twelve.'

In the dressing-room seconds later pandemonium prevailed. I was thumped on the back and jumped up and down. Everyone in various ways 'congratulated' me. One girl said she thought there could be no salvation for me, that when she heard me speak she was waiting for the thunderbolt of wrath to fall. Nothing like this had ever happened before. I had scored a sort of victory, which Marjorie had had the sense to take in good part.

As I've described the ballet school so far, it might sound as if we were all there under duress, as if we were working out some cross between a sentence to hard labour and an apprenticeship in one of the lowlier trades. This, of course, is how we liked to present it among ourselves, particularly the hard labour bit, but it was largely an elaborate camouflage for the enormous investment we had in what we were doing. Admittedly, not all of us were hoping to be professional ballet dancers; there were girls there who were preparing to be dance teachers in their turn, others whose performing aspirations went no further than summer show work, such opportunities for cabaret as came their way, and general variety work. But there were enough of us nursing high hopes of getting into ballet companies to tense up the atmosphere with criss-crossing jealousies and rivalries. In any case, whatever awaited in the big wide world outside, any ballet school develops its own system of internal competition and skirmishing for the rather scanty pools of limelight available. Promising friendships could sour rapidly as sudden progress pulled one member away into a coveted role, or even simply promotion to a more forward position in the lines of the ballet class, while the attention of visiting VIPs was madly coveted, madly resented when it went in the wrong direction.

Our greatest sense of solidarity emerged over exam times. I doubt if anyone wished even the most sworn rival the anguish of failing one of the dread RAD examinations. The examiners used to come up in pairs twice a year from London. During my student days Dame Adeline Genée, famous as a sparkling Swanhilda in the early years of the century, was still president of the Royal Academy of Dancing, and frequently appeared, minute and stately and terrifying, to examine. There was a rather touching system of helping each other change and prepare for these ordeals. Those who were not actually candidates, or had already gone through their exam a day or two previously, would accompany the victim to the scene of sacrifice, usually a strange public studio, help her into her tutu, and make sure tights were well hoisted up with the extraordinary block and tackle system of tape, elastic, and coins inserted into the material (it would require an elaborate diagram to explain fully). There might have to be a mad dash to the shops for extra packets of hairpins, a needle and thread; but mainly the task was to soothe and encourage, rather like seeing someone into the labour ward. The final ghastly touch was to have a large black number hung round one's neck, like a jockey, which sat crudely and incongruously on the satin purity of one's tutu bodice. My superstitions ran to three and multiples of three which I considered lucky.

At such times enmities were dissolved. When a harum-scarum girl flew goggle-eyed out of the examination room minutes after it had started with a broken shoe-ribbon we bled for her—although in less fraught moments we would have said in catty unison that it was a typical piece of Janie carelessness. A girl whom I had repeatedly sniped at for being slow on the uptake stood with her arms round my shivering shoulders, while I was waiting my turn to go in.

After the exams, inevitably, followed the results with a gap of four or five days. If the world was shining with success one kept a low profile out of deference to the weeping failures. The leaping around with joy and reprieve took place at home away from the studio. And within a week or two the whole matter was passed; one moved to a new position in the class and started working on the syllabus of steps for the next exam until the final Advanced examination had been passed. I had a clean run through, and by the end of my first year was thankfully quit of exams.

Our most frequent distinguished visitor was Arnold Haskell, who for a while took a lively interest in Marjorie's ballet school, and from the time I was twelve singled me out for gratifying special attention. However, his role in my career, which was considerable, is a confusing one and I regard him as a sort of *éminence grise* in my life. I never did know whether he spotted me as a promising dancer, or whether he was intrigued by this rather odd little misfit in the ballet scene. He certainly thought I was a girl of ideas and we used to talk long and absorbedly. He was also at that time plugging a rather peculiar line to encourage the recruitment of dancers. 'Time was,' he said, 'when the verdict was ''Oh, she's no good at school work, send her to ballet.'' But that,' he added emphatically 'is a lot of nonsense.' I'm not sure that I agree with him. In the interests of developing the well-rounded personality, obviously general education is important for anyone, dancer or otherwise. I would also be the first to complain, as I do repeatedly throughout this record, of the appalling narrowness of dancers' lives and interests. I'm not sure, however, that education or mental ability does anything for the actual quality of dancing. This depends, first and foremost, on a particular kind of body intelligence. It has nothing to do with whether one can string concepts together, or develop ideas in any other medium. The best dancers are highly intelligent, and musically sensitive. There are, however, legions of technically spectacular dancers who are musical imbeciles and mentally incurious to the point of being retarded. But they can do wonderful things with their bodies.

Leaving aside the question of talent, which in my case turned out to be moderate, I actually found it very distracting to be in the fortunate position of having several well-developed interests outside ballet. I didn't want to lose any of them, I was greedy. Part of my exhaustion came from trying to keep too many kettles on the boil, and I used to wonder uneasily in the privacy of my journal about the unmistakable connection between being thoroughly absorbed and happy in dancing and the lapsing of everything else—no books read, no music played no 'creative' work of any kind being done at home (nothing usually more venturous than a bit of dress designing or the odd scribble of writing). I still don't know the answer to the problem of narrowing down to one overriding commitment if temperament and upbringing have combined to produce an appetite for many kinds of stimulation.

51

Falling from Grace

The visit of the great god Haskell, for so we regarded him, to give his lecture on the solos from the *Sleeping Beauty* occurred towards the end of my first year. It was a minor triumph for me, coinciding with a fortunate upswing when I was working well and thirsting to shine before an audience. There is an element of luck in these things. My main rival, Maureen Bruce, actually a better and technically stronger dancer than myself, who went on to become a Sadlers Wells soloist, was feeling off form, subdued. With malice I noted that all her attention-seeking devices were failing, while I was absorbing gratifying amounts of the emiment critic's attention. She had the technically difficult Lilac Fairy solo to do, a much more testing piece of dance than the Humming Bird and the Crystal Fountain fairy dances which were my lot. But somehow that brief fluttering Humming Bird appearance, which Haskell introduced warmly as his favourite of all the fairy dances, brought the house down. There was a party afterwards at the home of a wealthy Edinburgh balletomane. High on a dab of gin and lime and the fulsome praises which were being lavished on me, I floated round that well-heeled gathering feeling I was taking my first sip of the celebrity life. Haskell talked long and earnestly to me about the Sadlers Wells school and the good education I would receive there. All the omens seemed excellent.

But tastes of the sybaritic life were rare. The usual kind of performance we gave was not in the plummy pretentious decor of one of Edinburgh's main civic halls, nor was it followed by gin and lime, soft lights and buffet suppers starting with oyster soup. Church halls, dance floors, schools, and those indeterminate rooms with a raised platform at one end which could be used for anything from a political meeting to a spiritualist's seance, were the usual venues, and if we got a cup of tea and a bun at the end of the show we thought we were being well treated.

As for those swings of fortune, I was hit by the reverse trend not ten weeks after the delirious Haskell visit. Dancing at a concert put on by some of my ex-school friends, I hit an all-time low, danced so badly that I couldn't even commit myself to the pages of my journal about it and spent a miserable fortnight

52

seriously wondering whether I should quit. To complete my mortification, on the evening of the performance whom should I spy, sitting four-square and ominous three rows from the front but Marjorie herself. This was an unlooked-for disaster. I'd agreed to dance at this concert as a purely private venture, and apart from being off form and giving a shocking performance, I had also put up a black by not informing her. In a set of oblique remarks spun out over several weeks, she led me to understand that it was not done to venture out on one's own, that if people wanted to dance outside her school they should tell her and she would choreograph a suitable dance—instead of people trying to perform solos which were too difficult for them. Not once did she speak directly to me, but the message came over clear and strong and unforgettably.

There was little time to brood. The Edinburgh Festival was at hand and with it the visit of the Sadlers Wells Ballet (later to become The Royal Ballet), with its full galaxy of stars, Margot Fonteyn, Pamela May, Violetta Elvin, Beryl Grey, Michael Somes. Marjorie's school was to supply accessories in the way of pages and peasant girls, mice and 'knitting women', for the sumptuous production of *Sleeping Beauty*, premiered the year before when the company, promoted to national status, had moved into Covent Garden. We were plunged into rehearsals with tiny, kindly Miss Kennedy, the assistant ballet-mistress, whose task it was to drill us in the various grandes promenades, peasant dances, and so forth. Even these minute slivers of prominence produced the usual reaction of strife. One girl, sulking because she wanted to be a peasant girl and not a mouse, brought in the heavy brigade in the form of a fearsome aunt, all gold curls and black shop-manageress suit, who came to 'see' Miss Kennedy about the affront to her niece. (Peasant girls had some actual dancing to do; mice did not.) Miss Kennedy, overawed, rearranged things and the girl got what she wanted—at the price of deep unpopularity.

The arrival of the Wells company caused a sharp polarisation among the inmates of the studio, neatly reflected in the arrangement of the dressing-room at the theatre, where we were ranged on either side of a long table divided by mirrors placed back to back. On one side were the gushers, older girls whom I scornfully nicknamed to myself the 'make-up and lipstick crowd'. Since two or three of them were soon to audition for the Sadlers Wells school, it is not so surprising that a certain amount of internal brainwashing was taking place, but I got heartily sick of the permanent delirium of appreciation, particularly about the company males—'awfully nice-looking on stage—', 'not a bit stuck up really', 'ever so friendly when you get to know him'. Most of it was ludicrous wishful thinking, if they were trying to fan the flames of romance, for it did not take a very perceptive eye to see that many of them were homosexuals, languid and effeminate off stage, and on stage bedevilled by that terrible prettiness of movement which spoilt much British male ballet dancing.

On the other side of the mirror barrier were the rest of us, hallmarked, I regret to say, by a kind of Edinburgh old-maidishness of attitude, a tut-tutting of disapproval against anything extravagant or outré. I belonged to it, partly because of the incessant swooning silliness of the other group. But my own reactions to the company were split in some discomfort between real dismay at their appearances—'effeminate fops of men and artificial girls' I wrote crisply in my journal—and deep admiration for the standard of dancing. With some relief I noted that 'Beryl Grey and Prokhorova (Violetta Elvin) look quite different'. As for Fonteyn, she was above criticism, on or off the stage.

But the fact remains, I never liked or warmed to ballet culture, was far too easily irritated by the camp mannerisms adopted by both sexes, was, in short, far too austere a character not to feel vaguely threatened by the atmosphere of posturing and gossipy chitter-chatter which I found time and again in ballet circles. To be truthful, it was excessively boring—but then most of what goes on in private group cultures is deadly boring, be it within academia, school staff-rooms, civil service canteens or within the so-called glamorous stage professions. I suppose that, as regards the Sadlers Wells, I had put them on a pedestal reserved for superior people, and was ill prepared to find them human.

However, the fortnight of their visit did constitute a 'high' bringing the usual sense of poignant finality when it was over. And it is still a unique memory, having watched Fonteyn from within several yards, not once but several times, dancing Princess Aurora. Of all the ballerinas who took the part that season only she retained the extraordinary sense of untouchable magic at close quarters. With the others, fine dancers though they were, that fragile membrane was broken and the machinery of technical 'management' introduced.

Finally, it was all over. 'The last night was a melancholy affair' I recorded. 'My partner in the farandole had the decency to say "Thank you very much". But . . . I never saw a soul to say goodbye to, not even Miss Kennedy. Margot Fonteyn surpassed herself. . . . The audience cheered and clapped and shouted "Bravo" for her. And when Betty and I went out of the Empire (theatre) she was standing inside the stage door and she gave us the most charming and beautiful smile. That is something I can treasure up. Betty and I walked home in the most profound state of depression which nothing could lighten until I induced her to come in (for five or ten minutes only, she said, but she stayed for two hours) and we had coffee and biscuits and a cigarette each, because we thought our nerves needed soothing. We talked and talked.'

So, with a see-sawing of excitements and doldrums, passed my first year as a ballet student.

Family Interlude

In the background, my family and its concerns remained the important counterpoint to the studio world, from which they were remote by several leagues. The gap was such that my brother turned ashen-coloured with fright when I told him I had enrolled him as a Ballet Club member, one of the rare instances when I successfully got my own back, and pulled *his* leg for a change.

My sister was by this time a medical student, and occasionally brought home dissecting room tales. But for the most part she was reticent about her university life. All we saw of it was the succession of admirers who appeared to fetch her out to dinner or dances or concerts, and for whom she prepared herself with meticulous care. Occasionally there were stilted suppers when one or other of them had been invited to eat with us, not markedly cheerful affairs, for my mother was still edgy and diffident about her cooking (learnt in the hard school of the time of severest rationing) and my father, none too happily embarked on his second and less exalted career in the home civil service, remained one of the most reserved though courteous of people. My mother has now for years been a quite excellent cook with a long-standing reputation for enjoyable hospitality. My father eventually retired from the civil service and went on to make a distinguished reputation for himself in town-planning and conservation. But in those days they were still fumbling for some *modus vivendi* with considerable strain.

I took a lively interest in my sister's love-life, as I had, rather intrusively, from the time she started having boyfriends. I had even set myself up as rival on one occasion when she brought home a dashing Polish airman whom I immediately coveted. So much did I covet him that I was convinced that his teasing gallantry and affection towards me were signs, on his part, of that grand passion which was lighting up my life. When I finally realised my disastrous mistake, I was so mortified at the foolish figure I had cut that love turned rapidly and irreversibly to hatred. The poor bewildered young man couldn't make out what had happened, why his adoring young admirer had suddenly turned savage, and tore up his letters—he had gone quite far in stringing me along—in his face.

I blushed over that incident for a long time. Nonetheless, I still continued to vet the talent Jill brought home with her, and thoroughly approved of her involvement with a muscular, rugby-playing, fellow medic called Donald. Indeed, in spite of the Polish airman affair, when Donald 'phoned up one evening and asked me to a concert, although incredulous, I accepted that it was possible I might in a modest way be included in a kind of shared relationship. I set out for the concert hall, dressed in my best dirndl skirt and new sandals, with high hopes, only to receive a powerful douche of cold water when I got there. For who should be waiting for me but a much less charismatic figure, a kind homely youth called Ronald, also an admirer, but a much less favoured one, of Jill's, whose name my wishful thinking had misheard. I'm not sure what he was doing inviting me to a concert anyway, unless it was his hopeful tactic to cement cordial family relationships, but, I'm glad to say, I behaved myself. That is to say, I accepted the situation graciously, and although lacking the savour of an outing with the god of the sports field, it was a gratifying enough experience to have been taken out by a real grown man.

As for my own emotional life, to be distinguished from the fragments I poached from my sister, it remained spasmodic and largely restricted to fantasy. I confided soft secret thoughts about a very young journalist to the pages of my diary—it might surprise him now to know the impact his blue eyes and clean-cut profile had on my fifteen-year-old heart. There was also a plaguing, teasing character at the Ballet Club who kept telling me to hurry up and grow up—underlining my perennial frustration at being too young for all the things I wanted to do. But for the most part I was delightfully untroubled. Real live boys of my own age, gauche teenagers, got a rather prim discouraging response to suggestions of dates or outings. With some truth, I pointed out I had no time. A brother of one of the girls at the studio did actually take me to two Friday night orchestral concerts, and then abruptly gave up. I wasn't even curious to know why, and only discovered something like twenty five years after the event—he had to remind me of our previous short acquaintance—that he found me too scaring. By taking up ballet we were, in fact, putting ourselves outside most of the normal situations where young people met up, school-based for the most part.

I lived a pretty solitary life without much companionship of either sex, to the extent that my mother sometimes worried out loud at my isolation. At that time, I didn't care. My family were all-important, particularly my father whose tastes I strenuously tried to cultivate in myself, some requiring no urging. I read books and enjoyed music without need of a model to emulate, though perhaps my excursions into some of the denser classics and Victorian writers were prompted by him. But his own particular passion for architecture I would certainly never have acquired without a wish to please, and despite the dubious motivation at its origin it has been an immensely enriching acquisition.

Yet somehow, in that over-intimate, over-protective setting of home, I had this real need to create something private and hidden, the journal, now two years on and becoming something of an obsession. Although I was, partly by nature and partly by the system of family role-allocation, the 'expressive' one, given to impulsive outbursts and, particularly with my mother, long emotional sessions of confiding, the secret world was a vital dimension. The journal entries are stilted and at least partly written under the surveillance of my official eye, the one that wanted matters to appear in a certain light and censored out admissions too painful to confront. Yet in a very real sense it was a place that I could retreat to, draw breath, and even if very tentatively at least broach some of the speculations, attempts at 'philosophising' about life, which were too tender by far to be admitted to family members. God plays a curious, stilted role in it. I appear to have been striving towards some kind of religious faith. But the ham-acting quality of my self-abasement in front of the Almighty's Divine Will is excruciating, and even now I can hardly bear to read my own words on the subject.

Far more important, though, than high or deep thoughts was an urgent desire to catch experience on the wing. I gave myself hell for not writing up events at the time, sure that recollecting them cold after a lapse of time was not nearly such valuable evidence. Evidence of what? I can't have known then how much I'd need that written reminder in later years to give me back, put me in touch again, with my own life. I can only think that I was trying to do what is nearly impossible, capture the freshness and immediacy of experience before it got staled over by conscious recall. I was trying to stay in touch with a source of vitality and spontaneity, which in myself was threatened by a too potent analytical consciousness, and in my family environment was similarly threatened by the atmosphere of rather terrifying watchfulness whereby we all turned each other into characters in a masquerade, the family game. The mixture of intimacy and game-playing which is the substance of most middle-class family relationships has been fully enough documented in psychiatric studies for me to be spared the need to sketch it in. All I need to add, with sorrow, is that enormous affection between members does not mitigate the crippling paralysis of emotional and creative energy which this peculiar deep falsifying produces. Making a performance of one's inner self, which the ethos of these intimate little structures insists on, is about the surest way of ensuring that the source of real creative self is reduced to a muddy spluttering in the dark.

My journal-keeping aroused a peculiar amount of irritation.

My mother said I spent far too much time on it,that I should set aside a fixed short time each day, if I must, and leave it at that. My brother got annoyed and scolded me if he 'caught' me at it—as though it were some form of furtive self-abuse. They were both reacting quite accurately to the fact that I was immensely self-obsessed. But as I've said, it was my attempt to make contact with both external and internal 'reality', for lack of a better word, quite as much as it was an extra exercise in narcissism.

In any case, there simply is a sharp divide between ruminants and others—people for whom experience is left hanging and confused until it has been re-invoked in some way, and those who can let it happen and slip by. It's true that the desire to preserve something of the quality of experience is in itself a destroyer. The very quality to be caught, if possible, on paper is too fine and good not to be broken by such an activity. When one's flying it's too much like breaking flight to stop and record it, which is why journals are often more eloquent when energies are turned inwards and life on the exterior is dull or uneventful, than when it's all go. Somewhere in her diaries Virginia Woolf remarked that these recordings reflected too much of certain moods. Ronald Duncan opens his autobiography *All Men Are Islands* with the sombre indictment: 'We settle down to write our life when we no longer know how to live it. To pause is to admit defeat. . . . We try to remember only when we've lost the vitality of doing anything worth remembering.' Anais Nin, that copious documenter of her own life, would say that by writing about it she created her life as it went along—yet the sneaking suspicion remains. Does recording siphon away precious energies for living?

Be that as it may, I was offending against a family norm by my recording activities. My father, though I do not remember him expressing open criticism about my journal, was not sympathetic to the idea of any kind of self-exposure on paper. He took a certain dry pride in being, as he said 'the only ex-Indian Civil servant not to write his memoirs'. It is a pity that he took that line—his memoirs would have been well worth having.

Years later, when I as a young adult confided to him that I wanted very much to write, he looked quite alarmed. 'Oh no, that's not a good idea,' he said, to my astonishment, 'To be a writer you'd have to become a completely different sort of person'. I'm still not sure exactly what he was getting at. I know that it means becoming a sort of exile in one's own society, a sentiment that's been expressed by innumerable writers in their different ways. But I think his alarm was over something rather different—that writing means commitment, to the best of one's ability, to a kind of honesty which stirs up things better left unstirred in the opinion of the majority, a defiance of the belief that the smooth surface is what counts above all things.

When I once put forward the view that it was harmful to conceal events of the emotional life he reacted with unusual vigour and told me to read the *Wild Duck* then I'd see the kind of chaos that resulted from a misguided desire to probe into hidden matters. I did read the *Wild Duck,* not so long ago. Where does it leave me? Confirmed in the compromise view that on the whole people are seldom strong enough to face and survive deeply threatening realities about themselves. Yet—I've seen too many instances of the inheritance of hidden fears, and of illusions that need elaborate stage-managing to persist. The issue remains for me full of foggy doubts.

Since I firmly believe that life is always lived at the symbolic or metaphorical level—that 'brute' reality would leave us with nothing to distinguish ourselves from the simple organic existence of appetites, survival, aggression, and death—the problem is to distinguish between more or less appropriate metaphors and scenarios for ourselves. Personal tragedies, in a society which more or less protects us from the starkest survival problems, are so often the result of misguided casting—by others in the first instance, then by ourselves, perversely undertaken to prove some obscure point, that we are different, specially gifted or specially doomed or simply the only ones who have got it right—all manner of dogmatic investments in testifying to some life view which we hold onto with clenched teeth and in the face of all evidence to the contrary. I am still locked in argument with my dead father about the importance of the life of feeling, although every venture I have undertaken on this basis has up till now ended in disarray. But I remain convinced that reason and emotion require to be well acquainted with one another, and that neither are dispensable.

After the Sadlers Wells' Festival visit, there were still two weeks of holiday, during which my father took my brother Mark and myself to Ireland, the first time I had been there since a barely-remembered interlude when I first came back from India. I fell instantly in love with Dublin, and underwent a rapid euphoric conviction of my Irishness, to which, since my father was a Dubliner, I could lay fifty per cent claim.

The remaining members of his family still lived in the old home, a modest red-brick house in the Rathgar district where his father had lived out his years as a mathematics fellow of Trinity College, and bred six children (one dead in infancy) by his tiny terrifying sabre-tongued wife. Irish Granny was something of a domestic Napoleon. She ruled supreme, a querulous despot with emphatic, not to say dogmatic views about everything. In fact, the family speech patterns, richly brogued, consisted of a series of defiant negative assertions about life and humanity in general, with particular reference to the deplorable characteristics of domestic servants, one of whom lingered on in the form of a dumpy country girl whose silence had the quality of stubborn disagreement and forced compliance with all her trying trio of employers.

For as well as my grandmother, there were the girls, Aunts Olive and Eileen, both in their forties, the former handsome, stone-deaf and grumbling, the latter a plain hairy infant of a woman permanently zareba'd against the outer world by the rich complexity of her obliging ill-health. There is always one aunt whose kisses one dreads. That was for us, by common consent, Aunt Eileen. Her spitty, moustachio'd embraces were moments of horror, terminated as fast as decency permitted. But the never-ending sagas of operations, and the lingering trauma-studded recoveries involving the villains and heroes of the medical profession, these were well past controlling. When Aunt Eileen sat down beside you with a particular eager look on her face, there was no escape. She was very small like most of my father's family, and from most seats her feet hung down not touching the ground. She would swing those dumpy little feet like a child, and like a child edge close to you till all those distressing hairs round her mouth were individually visible. And then followed the great epic of the unblocking of her Eustachian tubes, whose location was totally mysterious to me. Since this was usually followed by the hysterectomy story, I think I mentally placed them where it is more likely the Fallopian tubes are to be found. But whatever end of her malfunctioning body Aunt Eileen was so intent on delineating, it was all equally disagreeable. The less I knew about that shapeless little torso bundled under the layers and layers of hand-crocheted woollens in baby pinks, baby blues and pastel greens, the better pleased I was.

Under the general rosiness of that first post-war visit, even Aunt Eileen's big sheep-like head, with its giant horn-rimmed spectacles and grey-white woollen curls, was part of the general aura of beaming kindliness. While my father and brother put up at a hotel in town I was guest in the family home, and treated to all sorts of special attentions, like having my breakfast tray brought to me in bed, and the loan of Aunt Olive's prettiest fluffy bed jacket to put round my shoulders.

However, families are families and retain the characteristics hatched out in early life. The Russell household had never been famous for harmony. The womenfolk had argued and bickered their way through childhood and were still doing it. Something as simple as a rendezvous in town with the others could provoke a wrangling session with all battle lines and tactics revealed.

'OLIVE!' Aunt Eileen would bellow, 'We're meeting Edwin and Mark at *Bewley's* for lunch at one o'clock tomorrow.'

Aunt Olive would look up blankly from her book or newspaper. 'Were you saying something, Eileen?'

'BEWLEY'S' screams Aunt Eileen. 'We're meeting them at one o'clock.'

'Oh, Jury's, that's very nice,' says Aunt Olive, smiling vaguely and secretly, returning to her reading.

'Will yer *listen*,' says Aunt Eileen, climbing down from her chair and going over to her sister to shout the message in her face. Aunt Olive made considerable capital of her miserable afflicting deafness which had soured life since she was a young woman. When she wanted to be particularly aggravating—or found other people being so—she switched off her hearing aid.

'For the love of goodness, will you two girls stop this,' chips in their mother testily. 'Olive, you'll be at Bewley's at one o'clock sharp. Edwin doesn't like to be kept waiting.'

Olive nods to show she has received this message, but the next day keeps us all waiting forty-five minutes. My father is beside himself with exasperation, especially as my brother is playing the fool. At eighteen the whole excursion to Ireland makes him feel under duresse. He and my father get raggedly on each other's nerves.

I loved it all. Especially the food (we all enjoyed that) and the chance to buy clothes. This was the first sight of plenty within my effective living memory. Two fried eggs sitting on a field, roseate, of bacon rashers was Lucullan fare, not to mention the joints of meat my grandmother produced and the roast chickens washed down with sparkling hock and preceded with sherry. The good living undoubtedly coloured my fervently positive view of Eire, though I was also genuinely entranced with the loveliness of the countryside at Glendalough, south of Dublin, with its relics of an ancient Christian settlement.

Referring again to the fleshpots, I almost burst with pride and excitement at acquiring my first 'new look' costume, with bell-shaped skirt falling well below the knees, and a cashmere twinset to go with it—unheard of luxuries. There was some vague vestigial form of clothes rationing in Ireland, but often the matter of clothing coupons was waived aside in certain shops, or an obliging hall porter from the hotel would produce the cards of his numerous offspring or brothers and sisters for sale to visitors. My one fear was that at the Customs all these goodies would be wrenched off my back, including the new snug fur-topped boots bought as the finishing touch to my winter outfit, and I would be left shamed and shivering. After an earlier visit on his own, my father had told us of seeing a woman walking down the platform barefoot, her new footwear having been seized and confiscated. But when the time came, he ably steered us through the formalities, unperturbed by the threatening Customs notice thrust at him, while I trembled in the background in my new clothes.

With a mixture of real sadness and verbose sentimentalising I took leave of Ireland and Dublin. 'Oh Edinburgh, I am not unfaithful . . . for I have the affection of a friend for you,' I wrote on the last night, 'but for Dublin I have the affection of a child towards its parents'. There still was one last excitement to be tasted, the return journey on board a ship which I likened to a 'small floating palace'. 'The dining saloon was lovely with little mushroom lamps at intervals along the tables and chairs upholstered with dark bluey green. We had a last fling and all colours flying, so to speak, cold chicken and cider. Afterwards we went up on deck and watched all the shipyards passing by. It was sad to feel we were leaving Ireland further every minute. Daddy was sad too, and said very wistfully that Ireland gave him something that no other country gave him, and I know exactly what he means. After that we went down to our cabins and I had the fun of going to bed in my luxurious little cabin.'

Next day: 'With gathering gloom we made our way to Queen Street Station (Glasgow). Never have I realised how Scottish Scotland is! It is compared with Dublin and Glendalough so rigid and stiff. I suppose the thought of coming to austerity in everything also helped to heighten the effect, so I won't put all the blame on poor Scotland. . . . It was strange being back in dear old Edinburgh (the first and last time I think I have ever used that endearment) with its smoke-grimed buildings and long, colour-lacking streets. That's all I could think of, after the long rows of lovely shades of brick. It was bitterly cold too, another depressing factor . . . the winter smote one in the cheecks.'

And the next day I was back at the studio doing barre work and feeling my body strange and tentative after the long weeks of holiday, yet the pattern by this time was part of me. There was no quarrel, no inner or outer protest. I was by this time fifteen.

The Total Convert

As with any love affair which has ended in disarray and disillusion, it's difficult to relive completely the high moments, when one's happy passion is so sure and confident that there can be no doubts about the future. I never for one minute thought that a ballet career would be easy. I accepted then that my lot was to be continuous, striving hard work—and I did work enormously hard, too hard, some said. I wasn't even particularly confident of my talent. It was simply a case of knowing, then, that dancing was the most passionately important thing in life, that I was totally committed to it and that such commitment was almost bound to produce blossom and fruit.

It's an attitude to be found with despairing frequency among the devotees of ballet, a disease of dedication which blinds people to their own glaring unsuitability. In every dance studio I have ever worked in there are to be found, stumbling industriously in the back row, tucked humbly away behind the professionals, a handful of ungainly, overweight, knobble-jointed aspirers working with blind fanaticism to try and overcome the limitations of the wretched sheath which masks the soul within. They are doomed. Ballet is exquisitely harsh on souls. It demands them, all right, makes breakfast, lunch and supper of them. But they are worthless dross—unless their packaging is of that superlative and specialised quality which only the most unique and individual of talents can dispense with. There are a few dancers who have shone in ballet without beautiful arched feet, swan necks and long lance-like legs; but they are very rare.

I was not glaringly unsuitable. My body and limbs, although

not the perfect ballet prototype, were neat and pleasantly proportioned. I had a good line, quick footwork, and a fluidity of movement that netted praise. But my technique was never particularly strong, too easily upset by nervousness and tensions. My physical efficiency remained too much in the sway of an uncertain psyche, an unreliable ally, and never developed sufficiently its own realm of competence. There are various ways of describing 'technique'—one would be to call it a mode of functioning which is independent of personal inspiration. My dogmatism about the need for permanent inspiration was probably one of the main obstacles to consolidating a firm technique. All dancers have their quite dramatic ups and downs of development. Mine, I feel, were even more extreme. Progress was the outcome of some kind of manic elation; when the downswing of despondency came, everything seemed to crumble. There was little chance, under these conditions, of developing the necessary inner calm which is part of the basis for technical strength.

By this time I was not only a total convert to dancing, but to a very narrowly defined concept of dancing. I was now besottedly anxious to be a classical ballerina. At earlier stages, companies like the Ballet Jooss, with their much freer style and their break from formality into dramatic movement, had stirred me powerfully. I had not yet succumbed to the complete orthodoxy of the classical form. But in the same way that I crammed my feet into the straitjacket of point-shoes, ultimately damaging them, I narrowed down my ideals in dance. Feet and ideals alike seemed at the time quite well adapted to confinement; both started to give trouble later on.

Did I really think I could become another Fonteyn? Yes I did, in deepest most secret daydreams, and in the unknown company of hundreds of other teenage visionaries dotted over the ballet schools of the UK. Whether attainable or not, the supreme bliss was to envisage oneself poised on one point in arabesque, eyes turned towards the Holy Ghost, the elegant incarnation of pure and bloodless ecstasy. And to this end I strove, jettisoning whatever I started out with in the way of idiosyncratic pertness or sharpness. My days were spent obsessed with problems of placing, line technique. Schoolwork had been dropped once I'd passed my exam. I wanted to learn Italian, but was told it would be too time-consuming. Music also went by the board. It was nothing but dance, dance, dance.

The situation, however, was vastly more fulfilling than the grumbling crowded year before. By this time the three best dancers of the previous year had all successfully auditioned for the Sadlers Wells School. That left me in the middle of the front line at class and in the way of all the leading roles that were going, a state of affairs anyone would enjoy, and I did, to the full. Also, having made this definitive move from junior to senior student, Miss Middleton took on a different guise. The teacher-pupil relationship was now more co-operative, more respectful on both sides, though I must admit that I had never taken the worst swipes of her tongue, as some of the others had done. 'Clumsy cow!' she would shout at one plump bosomy girl whose shoe-ribbons were always coming undone, her bra showing, and her hair falling loose. Or 'Lift your bottom off the ground, you lazy cat!' to her bête noire, a girl with an exquisite face, a chest as flat as an ironing board, but over-ample hips.

These two, the inevitable whipping-boys, were not in their persecution united. 'Where does your cleavage start?' asks Katy, taunting her classmate about her lack of bust. 'Down at your navel?' 'Better than having one that starts under your chin,' retorts Jennifer tartly, glaring contemptuously at Katy's bulging front. And for the purposes of dancing she was right. A large bust was the very worst of afflictions. However carefully bound, the bodice of a ballet dress can't effectively support any more than the most vestigial of breasts. Those wonderful sweater-girl tits, streamlined into twin bomb-noses by the tough tailored cups of C-fitting brassières, would disappear into a sort of dismal cleftness cushion stuffed inside the low satin front of a tutu. So, however much one part of me envied the proud full busts of the womanly, the other, the dancer, the dedicated hermaphrodite, was thankful to be left unencumbered by any but the most token signs of puberty.

In my second year there were one or two changes in studio personnel. As well as Marjorie, there was for a pleasant few months a young woman called Miss Miles assisting with teaching. She was a dancer from Mona Ingoldsy's International Ballet company who had given up, I imagine, because her height was against her. Miss Miles was patient, authoritative and intelligent. Her manner was quiet and totally free from hectoring or bullying. She charmed us into hard work, and I valued the tips and insights she gave me about stage performing. She was tall, slender, cool and English with a page boy of blonde hair, a mallowy creamy skin and scarlet painted mouth, and she brought a refreshing touch of artistry into the sweat-factory of physical drudgery which a dance studio can so easily become. Unfortunately she did not stay long, leaving, I think, to get married, a highly likely outcome for someone so attractive.

We also acquired a different pianist. Class pianists are a species of underdog who have always claimed my curiosity, for they range from first-rate musicians making do until better things turn up to the lunatic fringe of the self-deluded, taking in hard-hitting efficiency and loud-pedalled inadequacy en route. I've already written a short story about the most unique, who appears later on in my experiences. But in the early years at Marjorie's, we had one or two who merited attention, particularly Mrs Barker, a tiny woman with bulging Pekinese eyes and frantic hair whose piano-playing gave the impression that she was always in the throes of a major artistic crisis. Imagine a mad mushroom, or a small button given to poetic dementia, and it will give some idea of the weird, agitated minuteness of Mrs Barker's hyper-sensitive persona. Marjorie called her a Biblical pianist, because she let not her left hand know what her right was doing. But Mrs B. was a good soul, and loyally sprayed the keyboard with her spidery passions, played every exercise as if it were a concert performance and exhausted herself happily on our behalf for many years. These were, of course, punctuated by the occasional trembling row when her ever-volatile emotions tried to turn into serious nastiness, at which times there seemed a real fear that she would fly to pieces. This usually occured after a performance for which she'd been playing, and in the heat of the moment turned over two pages of music, or reversed the order of the dances. With Mrs Barker at the piano, one had to be on the *qui vive* for emergencies.

Eventually, her place was permanently taken by a strange young man—or perhaps he was a strange elderly man—called Peterkin. I never knew whether this was his first or second name, but there was something faintly derisory about the appellation, whichever it was. Peterkin had a combination of iron grey hair and a high pink complexion, short legs and a long nose. He also had a mild speech defect which affected the pronunciation of the letter R. Like Marjorie's least favoured pupils, he was the butt of her bad temper, but unlike the former I don't think it overawed him in the slightest, although he followed her around like a rather dreary little court jester, attempting to crack his ponderous intellectualised jokes with little success. There was something indefinably irritating about him, a quality that provoked bullying. Marjorie shouted at him and we were quick to damn him for wrong *tempi.* He took it all too phlegmatically to rouse a pang on his behalf, and with an odd air of servile sniggering, as if he reckoned he had the last trick up his sleeve. And nothing cured him of his most irritating habit, which was to attempt to read a book while he was playing for class. The curious thing was that in spite of everything his criticism was respected. I, at least, felt that praise from Peterkin was praise indeed, and that here was a man who, whatever his deficiencies in self-presentation, had a genuine understanding of quality. Where he came from and how he had acquired his musical skill I have no idea. No one ever asked about pianists. They were the counting-house clerks of the ballet hierarchy.

The previous year Marjorie had made an attempt to lay the foundations for a ballet company. The details remain vague in my mind, if I ever knew them, but contracts were produced which she wanted our parents to agree to, whereby for a specified time we were committed to remain with her and not to look for employment elsewhere. She presumably had some reason to hope for financial backing before producing such a document, and was anxious not to see her best dancers dispersing south and become lost to her. None of our parents agreed to the terms, and no more was heard of the envisaged company. However, the Ballet Club production that year was much more ambitious than earlier efforts, no doubt with the idea of developing a repertoire suitable for a company, should it ever materialise. For the first time it included one of the classics of the standard repertoire, *Les Sylphides,* as well as works of Marjorie's own choreography. This year encouraged by last year's success, the classical revival was to be *Swan Lake,* Act II. We simply didn't believe her when she announced this. Overambitious folly! Even when she started rehearsing us, we didn't take it quite seriously, myself least of all, for she had cast me in the role of Swan Queen. I felt not only unready but unworthy. It was like daring to assume the part of the Virgin Mary with one's sins still all unpurged. I was also scared out of my mind at the possibility that she might go through with her intention.

For the first few weeks of rehearsals I stayed in this state of protective disbelief, that we were just playing at the situation. Then, one night, after a none too successful rehearsal with my partner, in which we'd stumbled and fumbled our way through the beautiful main pas-de-deux, I lay awake in bed, my mind racing through repeat after repeat of the day's events, as it often did when I was tired out. Suddenly, it stopped dead, stunned by a moment of piercing clarity. This dreaded event was really going to happen. I was going to have to get out in front of an audience and dance the Swan Queen. There was no make-believe about it, and no escape. I lay in bed panic-struck, crying with fright. But through that fit of tears some kind of resolve emerged. Immediate action must be taken. No more rehearsing in this slip-shod fashion, evading the technical difficulties and hoping they would mysteriously get better the next time.

The Total Convert

After I'd stopped crying I was determined on a course of extra practice. I would get hold of Bob, my partner, and arrange times when we would work by ourselves. For as well as sheer natural fright, I had a sense of *mauvaise conscience,* a feeling that I'd been holding back on the endeavour. I know that feeling well, a sort of retreat into protective inadequacy, a pouting protest to the almighty, or fate, that I can't be expected to do anything so tough or terrifying . . . and then, just as with the Swan Queen experience, comes the brutal moment of realising there's no let-out. And after rage and panic, some release of determination.

But as I am remembering that incident, it gets borne in on me how glad, basically, I am that I did not live out my life as a solo performer. To face that kind of situation, not once every now and then, but regularly, often—I wish I *did* have that kind of courage, but I haven't. Bravado is very exhausting for the timorous. And even with the amazing dazzling rewards of success, I'm still shocked at the price. Reading the autobiography of Margot Fonteyn, who, when I interviewed her in my role of dance critic a few years ago said (and I believe her) 'I've had a marvellous life', I was nevertheless awed by the impression of continuous fright in which she seemed to live. Her account of her career is singularly joyless, this greatest ballerina of the last fifty years. What comes over is, above all, the enormous sway exerted by other people over her existence, her fear and need to please such dragons of quality as Ninette de Valois, the agonising pressure of expectations. Fonteyn, if her own words are to be believed, still lived in a state of total precariousness about her own talents for years after critics national and international had poured their most poetic tributes into print.

Perhaps, as well as her marvellous artistry, some of her almost mystical appeal lay in the fact that she embodied one of the archetypal myths about dance—that it is the result of magical possession in both senses of the word, being possessed by the daemon of dance, but also by a master puppeteer, the most seductive expression of domination. The appeal is immense, the reality full of suffering. The fairy tale of the little mermaid

73

walking on feet that hurt as though she trod on knives is part of the same myth—passion as sacrifice and pain, above all something elicited by, or offered to, a grand and dominant being. Ballet is in many ways the fine flowering of the authoritarian spirit, and to that extent a sinister art. Enslave the body in certain ways of obedience, and mind and spirit will follow suit.

When I finally came face to face with my idol, Fonteyn, a quarter of a century after the days of her still rising star and my teenage adoration—that is to say, when she was in her mid-fifties and I in my early forties, it was a rude shock. She is reputed to have a mischievously evasive technique with the press and lived up to it. While I registered amazed admiration at the enduring beauty of her body and the crisp quality of trained energy which crackled from every purposive movement round the dressing room, I was chilled by her facade of humourless practicality, more so by her brisk gym-teacher manner of dismissing any question which asked for a considered response. The only subject on which she expressed herself with fervour was to deplore what she saw as the current fashion for protecting the young from taking risks that might be damaging to them. She had at least half a point. You do not learn through too much protection. The other half of the point, however, is that you do not learn, unless you happen to be both immensely gifted and immensely masochistic, by constant exposure to over-threatening situations. I would like to retain the belief that gifts can also be brought to full bloom without resorting to the methods of Sparta, that discipline does not have to be equated with self-punishment.

Fonteyn presented me with a paradox, a supreme artist entirely dedicated to what was *given* in her art. She seemed neither to question nor to want to innovate, showing no wish to be involved in either teaching or choreography apparently fulfilled in being the perfect responsive medium for others' ideas. Nevertheless, I felt humbled by her burning single-mindedness—also irritated that in her view the task of writing was light recreational stuff compared to the rigours of ballet class.

From the champagne of international fame back to the

homebrew of the ballet school. Rehearsals for the production of *Swan Lake* were interrupted over Christmas for a performing interlude much more lighthearted. Marjorie's school always supplied the dancers for the pantomime season at Perth, with its bijou Victorian theatre like a scaled-down miniature of an opera house. The pantomime was a riotous piece of light relief for the hardworking repertory company, which has in its time hatched out notable performers—Donald Pleasance, John Gregson, Gudrun Ure and many others, who learnt their stage-craft on Perth's diminutive boards. For Marjorie's dancers, the whole three weeks had the magic of a pantomime transformation scene. A wand had been waved, and we were translated from the dinge of the studio to the real live excitement of the stage, mixing with real live actors, with real money (though very little) being paid to us. It was an event which had already gathered a glitter of anticipation from the accumulated lore of good times, romantic encounters and stage adventures from previous waves of students, all of which, with miraculous repetitive fulfillment came one's way when the great moment arrived, and, as one of the select group of eight senior students (two boys, six girls), boarded the train for Perth.

Dancing in the panto was not simply a question of brushing up on tap routines and supplying the chorus line. There were three 'spots' of our own, miniature ballets, one a Sylphides-type white ballet in which I took the lead, another in which I had a quaint little solo as a wooden doll mourning its lack of colour among all the other toys, and an 'oriental' ballet in which we all swooned around in harem pants and Jennifer of the exquisite slant-eyed face took the lead. We thought our little ballets were very important, and plenty of adrenalin flowed when it was our turn to be on. Nowadays (still under Marjorie's seventy-year-old direction) it is all much more casual. The dancers recruited for the purpose are not aspiring ballet dancers but girls who dance commercially in pantomimes or summer shows as a means of earning a temporary living. But in the good old days Perth supplied a sort of nursery slopes situation for those with hopes of solo status on larger stages.

The three weeks spent over Christmas and New Year had the hilarious improbable quality of a schoolgirl story set in a theatre. Most of the girls shared digs in town, but one other girl and myself, considered too young and tender to be entirely without supervision, were booked into a double room in Marjorie's hotel. I was horribly disdainful of my companion to begin with. She was quiet and withdrawn and colourless, even her back expressing meekness and indecision. Her commonest remarks were 'I don't know' or 'So do I', and I have a nasty feeling that I gave public vent to my dismay at having to share a room with her for three weeks. Anyway, in the event, I had to eat my words. Behind her pallid reserve, there lurked, when it dared to peer out, a rather engaging sense of humour. We pooled the goodies which our mothers faithfully sent from home to supplement the barren hotel fare and had many a midnight feast, often in the company of visitors from Edinburgh, for loyally the students who were not in the panto came up to see us perform. Sometimes Marjorie and the faithful Peterkin brewed tea in the night-porter's scullery and brought it up to our room. At others, we were joined by her teenage son and daughter and the long sprawling sessions of gossipy analysis of personalities and performances, on and off the stage, would go on into the small hours, all of us wound up tight with excitement and unable to sleep. Other nights, exhaustion caught up and we would throw ourselves into bed, hardly taking time to wash the remnants of greasepaint from our faces.

We were hard-worked and short of sleep and high the whole time, hooked on that time acceleration which is the lure of politics, gambling and being in love, and stage productions above all, when the configuration of life chances changes almost by the hour, and destiny darkens and shines with the erratic speed of a bulb with a faulty connection. The ups and downs of our own performances were interlaced with shifting alliances and rejections among our own group and increasingly with the actors of the company, with whom we started to fraternise. Among ourselves we bitched and snarled as per usual, but there was also a feeling of group solidarity—us dancers, as distinct from the actors, whom I think we all felt had a relatively easy time of it compared to us.

Yet the whole atmosphere was festive. On Christmas Eve a group of actors and dancers went to a tiny church somewhere on the outskirts of the town to hear midnight mass, a brief and rare experience of heart-lifting peace. Nothing seemed easier at the time than to gather all this lovely gang of people into a great embrace of effortless warm fellow-feeling. Never had people seemed so lovable, myself so full of generosity. It wafted us back down to the town, this gladness, and hung around in the crisp frosty night, and added something special to the ravenous hunger with which we tore into hot dogs bought from a solitary stall miraculously open at that hour. Still in this state of unusual goodwill we wandered through the deserted streets and wished each other 'Happy Christmas' when the day was only two hours old. Next morning, late, Marjorie entertained us in her hotel room to sherry and cake and presents, and gleamed benevolently at us through her spectacles. Four hours later, after a shocking matinée, she was tearing into us for slovenly work and immediately posted up a notice for class and rehearsal.

As the three weeks progressed, I mellowed and expanded in the sun of flattery and compliments that came flying my way, delightful and reassuring. My parents and brother and sister came up in relays to watch me perform. Various unnamed adults talked to me intently and seriously about my 'future'. Best of all, in its mild way, was to be told by some of the actors that I had started to relax on stage, to 'project' pleasantly and unbend from the tight-lipped seriousness of the first performances. 'I shall miss your absurd little doll dance,' one of them said on the last night.

And just so that all the facets of existence should be seen to gleam with equal promise, romance blossomed with startling unexpectedness at the eleventh hour. At that time I was happily poised between curiosity and unconcern with regard to the opposite sex, casting an appraising eye over the men without any anxiety about making a catch. How I rated as a dancer was infinitely more important than my standing as a woman. But increasingly towards the end of the run I found myself having long talks in the wings, or over late meals in the nearby Italian restaurant, with one of the actors, a curious shaggy older man of twenty-eight who showed marked interest in my work and whose intensity about his own sounded a common note between us. Jimmy, I discovered, was a latecomer to the profession. He'd walked out of a civil service job to take to the boards. He had a leonine mane of hair, a sharp frownline like a geological cleft in his forehead, and as I discovered when he wore the kilt, which he did taking the part of Lachie in *The Hasty Heart,* rather good legs.

It was in fact after watching a rehearsal of this classic tear-jerker, about a dour Scots soldier dying of an incurable disease and finally finding himself able to accept the human love and friendship he had rejected all his days, that some kind of special rapport developed between Jimmy and myself. The play is of the kind that is rightly discarded as cook-book sentimentality when one attains the years of critical maturity and cynicism. At fifteen, I along with the rest, found it a poignant experience. Rather more so than the rest. To my embarrassment, I found the tears splashing down my face as I watched. Worse still, someone noticed them and the buzz immediately got around that Una had actually wept while watching the rehearsal. Jimmy came hotfoot to find me and check up that this was true, amazed and very gratified when I admitted, not very willingly, that his performance had moved me to tears. 'I can't get over it,' he kept saying, 'You always seem so aloof and dispassionate!' Had he but known it, he was telling me the story of my life, a permanent contradiction between the raw emotions swirling away inside and a misleadingly contained exterior presenting to the world.

Anyway, thus encouraged, Jimmy followed up our burgeoning friendship with an invitation on our last Sunday in Perth, when the final performance had been given in a glow of last-night goodwill, to go for a walk with him. We talked and talked, about me, about him, and about the stage. He praised my dancing and said he would come to Edinburgh some time to see how I was

progressing. Rather to my surprise, he did. We had a few
snatched interludes in the nearby milk bar between Ballet Club
rehearsals on Sunday afternoons, manoeuvring our way into
temporary privacy with difficulty, for it was not done to depart
too openly from the fiction that his visits were part of the
continuing cordiality between Marjorie's dancers and the Perth
company which survived the memorable panto season by a few
weeks. Over cups of weak coffee we gazed at each other, I,
embarrassed and flattered and friendly but not otherwise too
much affected, he, temporarily in the throes of something more
disturbing. What I had to offer was nothing much more than
schoolgirl affection. But Jimmy, almost twice my age, was
writing nine page letters, and asking me to come up to Perth to
see him, he would pay for me to stay at a hotel. My mother,
however, intervened over this particular plan (which I doubt was
a calculated seduction, or am I still being naive?) and Jimmy
resorted to 'phone calls and yet more letters instead. They were
very lively and entertaining, and I contrasted my stilted replies
very unfavourably with his easy conversational flow.

He came again, to watch a Sunday rehearsal (at which I danced
very badly, unnerved, I suppose, by the fact that he was watching,
my critical adorer), and afterwards we went once again to the milk
bar. The atmosphere was tense with unspoken feelings.

'The whole thing's absurd' he said, over and over again. And
then asked what was for so long the fatal question: 'How old are
you?'

'How old do you think I am?' I countered.

'My most pessimistic judgment puts you at about fifteen,' he
said. And again: 'The whole thing's absurd! Fancy a man of
twenty-nine coming miles on a train to see a girl of fifteen!' But
this time he swept on. He wanted to see my parents, making sure
I realised what a bizarre move this was for him. What on earth did
he have in mind? Some years' long engagement? I waited,
praying with part of me for life and Jimmy to revert to normal,
with another, on edge for what would happen next.

At this point, a gang of others from the studio joined us, and we started talking very fast about films we'd seen. And here some ambiguity about Jimmy's movements creeps in. He had to catch a train back to Fife, because he was staying at the home of one of the other ballet students. What was he doing there? Perhaps the company was performing in the vicinity, perhaps not. Perhaps he was a low two-timer, having a normal affair with Katy of the large bust while he slaked or inflamed his higher passions with me. I don't know. But there was this urgency about catching trains. Jimmy started asking desperately if there wasn't a later train he could catch. Katy looked distinctly cool at the idea, and it was dropped. The three of us went down to the station where Katy discreetly disappeared into a carriage leaving Jimmy and myself standing gazing at each other on the platform.

'Talk to me,' he said, holding both my hands. 'I don't mind what it's about, just keep talking.'

I did, about the studio, about my family life, while he stared and stared at me. I started to feel uncomfortable. 'Why are you looking at me like that?' I asked finally.

'It's nothing,' he said. 'Go on.' But I had hardly started to speak again before he'd interrupted with his usual lament. 'It's so absurd—you know what I'm getting at?'

'Sort of,' I mumbled, and feeling I had taken a large step too far immediately added: 'But I just want to be friends.' The fatal clanging platitude—only in this instance more than half sincere.

'Friends,' he said, hollowly, the actor busily taking over. He looked away with dramatic disappointment.

'Have I said something nasty?' I asked anxiously.

'No—but I'm suddenly rather depressed and neurotic,' and with that he started saying farewell in every language he could think of—French, Italian, German, and what I took to be Russian.

'Not *adieu*,' I said, latching on to the one familiar tongue. 'Just *au revoir*.'

'I don't know, God knows when I shall see you again.'

Another agonised pause on my side. The situation was positively operatic. But suddenly it dissolved into pure intimate tenderness. He leaned forward and kissed me full on the lips, very gently, there on Waverley platform with the guard banging the train doors.

'You are very sweet,' he said, almost soothingly. 'And I shall try and come to see you as soon as I can.'

That kiss stayed with me like a brand mark for several days, accompanying me as I went about my everyday business, rising clear and evocative to the surface in quiet moments, as I sat musing about the strangeness of it all, feeling a most unaccountable stirring in my body every time I recollected it. It had me sorely troubled. Should I or shouldn't I have let it happen? Part of me treasured it. Another part wanted to dismiss it briskly, as totally out of line with the wholesome concept of 'friendship' which I clung to. Another, less high-minded, reaction was to fear that I had put myself on a par with the other girls, who had no ungodly investment of pride in concealing their partiality for particular men. I suppose I still had in the back of my mind that collection of photographs which my grandmother had once shown me, of all the young men who had been sweet on her. 'And I never let one of them kiss me' she had told me with quiet pride. I was definitely falling from family standards of good conduct.

Jimmy continued to write; he did come to visit me at home, an event I anticipated with a silent scream of dread because my hyper-critical family would now be in a position to pass judgment on my swain. It passed off pleasantly enough. He ate lunch with us. We went for a walk in the neighbourhood, conversing affably and as platonically as I could have wanted—except for one bad moment where he said something about 'laying his head on my bosom' and glanced down at my almost invisible breasts. I felt he was making obscure fun of me, confusing me with his mixture of sarcasm and tenderness. That visit must have pointed out to him the absurd difference in our life-stages, let alone our ages. We continued to exchange letters spasmodically, but that, effectively, was the end of the thing I was so anxious should not turn into an 'affair'.

There have been no more older men in my life since Jimmy, for which I'm rather sorry. I think I might have enjoyed a father-figure as lover or husband. Instead, the theme which that first incident could have sounded has been turned upside down. From my mid-thirties I seemed unavoidably to get involved with men half a generation younger than myself. For someone as hung up on symmetry as myself, life seems to have decreed a permanent lesson to the contrary.

Swan Lake and After

All the rest of that winter dancing continued to fill the horizons and the messages about my work, both from my own inner monitor and from other people, were that it was going well and I was progressing steadily. This, despite the fact that I failed the Solo Seal, a tough exam which had necessitated a visit to London. However, the verdict was softened to some extent by the examiners' comment that I showed much promise, and the fact that Frederick Ashton had spotted me as worthy of attention. The trip, examination ordeals notwithstanding, had that quality of spree which my rare visits to London continued to have until I went to live there.

Experiences were fairly sharply contrasted. On one side was the usual hard work and the scary business of being up for appraisal before alien eyes—and how alien they can be! The secretary of the Royal Academy of Dancing (under whose auspices the exam was conducted) was then a large and rather formidable lady who eluded all my attempts at categorisation. She was broad of build, imposing, eternally black-suited, with a deep drawl, a cigarette permanently aslant in a long holder, and had a manner which combined extreme sophistication with a certain back-slapping heartiness. On the occasion of the Solo Seal I read my changing fortunes in her all too eloquent eyes. Coming off after my first solo, which had gone well, she was all over me, alight with enthusiasm. During the second solo I made an unfortunate stumble. A pair of glazed pebbles stuck in a blank disinterested face looked past me as I came off stage, forewarning me that I had tossed away my chances of passing.

Miss Lehmann belonged to that maddening group of lay people who nevertheless had the knowledge and the right to weigh one up as a dancer. I've always had a rather strong reaction against what I privately called 'ballet hangers-on'—quite unfairly in her case, since she fulfilled a perfectly legitimate and necessary function. But the sight of ungainly people, leading safe unchallenged lives within their sheltered bodies, passing judgment on our exposed physical existence, always irritated me. This feeling extended to critics and others, men and women who were vaguely 'around', and who had mysteriously established a sort of right to be present at ballet events and to pronounce on what they saw. There was a hint of voyeurism about it, of a kind of feeding on flesh, long before the manifestation of more recognisably declared interests in the said flesh. Later, as a company member, I realise how lowly they were rated, these camp-followers (not, of course, bona-fide power-wielding critics), how little they seemed to be aware that we thought they cut rather comic figures, in spite of their invitations to supper and their flattery.

The other side of my London visit was an unusual taste of sybaritic existence supplied by old Dublin friends of my father's, a brother and sister, both unmarried, who lived with great attention to their creature comforts, even in the lean post-war years. Their hospitality overflowed with the good things made possible by Uncle Frank's lucrative practice as a medical consultant, and I was positively awe-struck by the electric bed-warmers (pre-electric blanket devices like large metal cushions inserted between the bed-clothes), the wine and the good food, Frank's magnificent record player and vast library of records, the frequency with which they dined out at restaurants, and the grand circle tickets for Covent Garden and Drury Lane. In fact, one's system could be over-taxed with all these goodies. My brother has a ghastly recollection as a small boy of throwing up at the end of a school outing with these munificent godparents, when they had fed him with every rich thing available, finishing at the end of a marathon of gluttony with strawberries and cream.

Nothing so disastrous happened to me, but I too remember feeling pale and wretched after over-indulgence in rich food, of spending feverish sleepless nights after unaccustomed amounts of wine. A test of stamina of a different nature was presented by Frank's semi-joking, semi-inquisatorial testing of one's knowledge and discrimination. At the end of a sublime piece of music, which I had been dreamily absorbed in, would come the jolting question: 'Now, Una, who is the composer of that piece?' Confounding Mozart with Bach—a fairly basic error of judgment, I'll admit, but good God, at fifteen is it a crime? Is it ever a crime?—would produce such a feeling of embarrassed failure that I could only squirm back deeper into the cushions of the enormous chair or couch I was sitting in, lower my eyes, and wish that I could disappear. There was no malice in it, nor yet in the quizzings about my knowledge of London streets when we went motoring. Having taken me a particular route once before I was supposed to have retained some eidetic imagery to which I could refer for all time. Since I had a terrible sense of direction, this was another sure victory for my questioner. It was, of course, a sort of game, perhaps even intended to instruct and improve, but I did not enjoy these repeated demonstrations of fallibility even with such a jovial omniscient as Uncle Frank.

But these are minor matters, compared to the fact that these kind people provided me with a home from home when I went to live in a London hostel, that they asked nothing in return and entered into no emotional bargains. They were warm-hearted and practical and straightforwardly loved their food and their entertainment, and were ready to share it open-handedly with people they were fond of.

Meanwhile, back in Edinburgh, time was running out before the Ballet Club performance, with *Swan Lake, Apocalypse,* a new ballet of Marjorie's based on the Revelations of St John with striking costumes by Valerie Prentice, a London designer, a repeat of *Les Sylphides,* and some small divertissement piece based on Degas' familiar painting. Fully occupied with the three others, I had nothing to do with *Apocalypse,* and cannot remember enough about it to tell if it's fairly venturesome theme was well realised or not. I was working as hard as I knew how, swinging as ever between exaltation and dreadful doubts, but basically carried along by a high tide of energy.

I imagine that anyone, amateur or professional, who has had the experience of putting their all into a particular role knows of the curious bubble-state in which one lives, a peculiar and very special sense of containment in which everything else drops away. Though my world was very small at the time, I had the exquisite satisfaction of knowing and feeling that I was at the centre of it, not simply because I was taking a leading part but because I and what I was doing were completely aligned. No gaps between watcher and doer.

And yet at the same time I have never been, I think, more completely passive and dependent in my life. I floated on the love and hope of my parents and my teacher, a kind of vessel for the aspirations of others. I think it is an experience which many young girls go through, of being an embodiment of poetry, inspiration, of catching up through their own delectable quality of formless potential all sorts of nebulous desires from others. I'm reminded of the strange passage in *The Glass Menagerie,* when the calculative mother of the crippled heroine suddenly bursts into a pathetic lyrical reminiscence of her own young girlhood, of how for a short season she, now shut into a thankless hard-worked existence, floated in poetry and gossamer gowns through the springtime, gathering jonquils, jonquils everywhere. And what follows, almost inevitably? A lifetime of feeling subtly cheated, unless one has the sense and strength not to go on sipping at the thin nectar of nostalgic memories. And yet—there's no gainsaying the fact that the high moments of fulfilment, whether in art or love, through beatific distortion or otherwise, *are* the unbeatable experiences, and cannot, perhaps should not, be forgotten.

We had one important visitor to the studio during the rehearsal period. This was Ram Gopal on what must have been his first tour to Britain after the war. I had gone twice to see him perform at the Usher Hall, and found this first experience of Indian dance magical beyond words, a meeting point of sensual beauty and mysticism. I believe that from the purists' point of view, Ram Gopal was to be faulted for a degree of westernising in the presentation of his dances. There are times when it is more rewarding to be ignorant. I spent two evenings of complete enchantment, and would thoroughly endorse the present *Encyclopaedia of Dance and Ballet* entry, in which he is described as a 'dancer of extraordinary beauty' and a 'lucid talker as well as a brilliant performer'. I found him all those things, and the excitement of his visit to our studio was barely dimmed by the fact that this radiant god, on closer inspection, was not quite as untarnished by time as he appeared on stage. For whether remote in the glow of stage-lighting, supporting his enormous gilded head-dress, or close to, with slightly thinning hair and dark glasses, he remained a charismatic figure. Marjorie introduced some half dozen of us after we had shown him some of the ballets we were rehearsing. I danced the pas-de-deux from *Swan Lake,* at the end of which he applauded loudly and told me, as I shook his hand, 'You are a lovely dancer and I have enjoyed watching you'. It is the only piece of praise which still gives me a small thrill of pleasure.

Of the actual performances of *Swan Lake* and the other ballets, very little needs to be said. It was, with a little additional glamour, the same kind of experience as being head-girl or boy of the school, captain of cricket or tennis, a moment of glory that is, by the system, bound to be handed on to a successor, magnificent and epic while it is being lived. I was immensely touched when Maureen, my old rival, and now translated to higher things in the Sadlers Wells second company, sent me a bouquet wishing me good luck. It showed, I felt, that in spite of her advancement she had not forgotten that testing oneself in the little world before venturing into the large, can still feel like standing on the steps of the high dive.

It was a gorgeously emotional time. On the last night I received a bouquet from all the boys in the Club, which, considering my sometimes acid relations with them and the usual rehearsal history of huffs and moods which affected us all from time to time, brought me to a state of easy tears. My partner and I had, of course, almost persuaded ourselves that we were in love but that withered healthily and quickly back to everyday friendship almost before the last night party was over.

But it was my family's enthusiasm, particularly my sister's, that touched me most deeply. She and I were by this time very fond of each other. She was no doubt happily enough involved in her own vastly different kind of life to let drop the old irritations over my appetites for limelight, yet I was taken aback at her wholehearted pleasure in my success. It was, in fact, a time for family celebration for my brother had just won a scholarship to Oxford, and we all dined out in style one evening to mark this double achievement.

Swan Lake wasn't quite over by the final performance. The very next day we spent twelve hours at the theatre being filmed for a documentary that was being made about Edinburgh. *Waverley Steps,* not the most brilliant of films, recorded for a few years my dancing as Swan Queen in a few brief snatches interspersed with scenes of the student hero and heroine jitter-bugging at a 'varsity hop and necking discreetly on a park bench. My sister, who had a funny knack of picking up on my life at unexpected moments, saw it several years later in a backstreet cinema in Liverpool. But that is the last I heard of it, and I suspect it's just as well.

By this time my two years at the Edinburgh studio were nearly over, and decisions had to be taken about the future. It is strange how little I know or took part in the actual taking and shaping of these decisions—why I did not audition for the Sadlers Wells school, for example, but went to study at Idzikowski's studio in London, as a solitary venture. My father was anxious that I should audition for the Sadlers Wells, that most exclusive of ballet establishments, with, I think some idea that it would be a fairly decisive indication one way or the other of the kind of talent I had. In retrospect, I wish I had, for just the same reasons. It would have been a testing at a crucial time not only in the career of a ballet student but in a person's life. If I had got in, it would have put me in the way of the best as well as the most rigorous training available. If I had not, then I would have had to pause and think out whether my wish to continue in ballet was strong enough and my faith in my own abilities able to withstand such a setback.

I suspect that it was a test my mother couldn't face. There was too much at risk. For, in spite of her pride in her other two children, my dancing was a vital element in her life. It must have sounded deep in her some note of disowned poetry, for she insisted on presenting herself as someone incapable of 'appreciating' culture or art at any depth, an earthbound creature compared to all us aesthetes, especially my father and myself, who were supposed to have a kind of permanent plug-in to the Higher Things of life. But my mother is a passionate woman, if not an imaginative one. Unhappily for herself and for me, she never trusted herself to bring this emotional intensity to the surface through any channel of her own finding. Convinced of her own lack of creativity and constantly denying her powers of appreciation, she turned to others to do it for her. She read voraciously, but was always convinced she had not got the right things out of her books. She enjoyed music, but never 'understood' it the way we did. At one time she played the piano well, but gave that up in discouragement at her facing technique. Her mind, which was perfectly capable of both sharpness and logic, she gave over to be directed by my father, whose opinion and judgment she adopted almost unfailingly—except when she badly wanted her own way. It is an old story, and a sad one, of a woman with immense energy and drive determined to defeat herself and live by proxy. It is also one of the strongest arguments for Women's Lib. that I know.

In my 'teens I was immensely fond of my mother. I asked nothing better than to share my life with her—hopes, discouragements, triumphs, excitements, fantasies. It never occured to me to hold back, I had no self-saving sense of reticence—which was perhaps why I had to dig myself a little deep pit of privacy in that journal. I felt myself wafted high on her enormous devotion. But increasingly over the years I started, only half consciously to begin with, to make over the truth into what she wanted and needed to hear. The possibility of my failure to live up to our shared expectations of artistic and social success was too threatening to be faced. I dared not lose face in front of her, by this time anxiously if inarticulately aware that I was a source of some rather desperately needed sustenance.

For long enough I found it gratifying. To be someone's inspiration is an old devil's temptation, Galatea giving back some of her own joyous freedom to a weary Pygmalion, perhaps enjoying the role-reversal, perhaps even overlooking the fact of being still a creature of the old creator. Eventually the strain of this double version of self became acute, a matter of performing my core self while I was still trying to discover it. As in many families with destructively close ties, we trafficked in raw material—'deep' emotions, honesty, sincerity and so on, while at the same time practising a fearsome concealment. We cracked down on more innocent and overt forms of performing, the normal fun or simply normal protection that people assume by exaggerating their social behaviour. 'Posing,' being 'artificial', mannerisms, these were all moral failings and time-wasting deviations from the business of real, straight communication. So they are, but one cannot be hand-on-heart honest twenty-four hours a day. In any case, honesty is a subtle and difficult practice, quite different from the kind of confessional attitude which was my mother's version of honesty. What I am trying vainly to pinpoint is a quality of deep evasion, deep adulteration in these very personal feelings which we exchanged, because the aim was *not* 'straight' communication, or openness, but the old business of making over the reality of experience, at whatever price, in order to hold a threatened private world in one piece. And in that I colluded, with some degree of awareness as I grew older, while she, I rather think, had none.

Perhaps the saddest thing of all is that she had not the first idea how to handle that lively, deviant streak in herself, the force which reacted intuitively and positively, during her days as a memsahib in India, against the indifferent, lazy superiority of many Englishwomen to their Indian surroundings and servants. Which gave her the courage to send us to Moffat Academy rather than the select private school. Which fed her interest, although somewhat matriarchally expressed, in the people, labourers and artisans. Which may indeed have nudged her into that dismal period of semi-slumming when we first came to Edinburgh. In many ways the most loyal of professional-class members, in others I suspect much resentment at the terrible boundedness of class mores.

Just how involved she was in my career as a dancer I did not realise until I went to London, a sojourn which started out full of promise.

London

Fairfield Lodge, where I went in the autumn of 1948 to live for the next few months, was the training centre for a professional course in ballet teaching run by the Royal Academy of Dancing, as well as serving as hostel for a few professional dancers. It was a large Victorian house in a quiet avenue in Holland Park, set back from the road by a short drive bordered with dark-foliaged shrubs, its main attraction the big common sitting-room with French windows giving onto a wide lawn at the back of the house, where, among other things, the annual RAB garden party was held.

Living there, I was in a category by myself, being neither a trainee teacher nor a working dancer, and I have been in this position, or one of a tiny minority, more or less ever since; only British girl in a French ballet company; widow at twenty-eight; university student in my thirties; the great romance I never had in my teens at forty; dropout from secure employment at the age of forty-three. There is some weird theme of mistiming, all the more comic since I have in part at least a strong desire to find myself in the dead centre of conformity, if only for safety's sake. Yet unfailingly fate, or some imp of deviance quite outside my control has always pulled the rug out from under such aspirations, if they can be called that.

My first reactions to Fairfield were eclipsed by an agony of homesickness. Life for the first few days, if not weeks, was simply a vale of tears. 'I really feel a new chapter is starting, and yet I am in terror of closing the old one' I wrote in the faithful journal, a large tome handsomely bound in brown with beige leather corners and spine and thick quality paper, which I had found as a fabulous bargain at a time when paper was in short supply and mostly of the dreadful squashed porridge variety. Along with a dozen books selected more as symbols of shared culture with my father than anything else—poetry, architecture, Shakespeare's plays—it was all that I had to remind me of home.

'All my fine ambitions . . . are brought to nought by the persistent desire to live my life selfishly and merely be happy in the secure company of people I love. I suppose it's because I'm going off on my own rather young . . . that has rendered me so clinging and dependent. There are no common denominators—except myself, and that is such an unstable one. Dancing should be the other, but that takes on a new complexion here. . . . In fact at this moment I am utterly and completely bewildered. . . .' A fairly typical reaction to the terrors of moving from pond, to main stream, if not actually the ocean deep.

This state of collapse, thank goodness, did not last long. I started to enjoy my dancing classes and also the novelty of being part of a community of girls and young women, united, if by nothing else, in an antagonism which was more good-humoured than vicious against the hostel authorities. 'They' were the warden, an ex-WRNS officer, slightly weatherbeaten, upper class, and not much in evidence, and an ex-ATS ranker, freckly with lank pale ginger hair and a dull papery complexion, who was in charge of catering, by common consent voted abominable. In fact, much of social life was geared round the sharing of extra food in the form of contributions sent from home, or outings to cafes in Kensington High Street for a fill-up on buns and cakes. At weekends many of us disappeared off home or to relatives to be stoked up on food and affection.

For me, the meagre hostel diet was lavishly supplemented by the hospitality of my father's Dublin friends, and also by that of his youngest and only married sister, who lived at Streatham. I have to confess that food was by far the strongest motivation for my visits to Aunt Caroline, although I became very fond of her, for her domestic life was both boring and harassing. She had married at forty, after a mysterious career lived on the fringes of Bohemia, from whence floated vague tales of foreign lovers and quite untypical irregularity for a member of my father's family; and her choice had fallen on quite the dullest man I have ever met.

Unlike many dull people, he did not have the grace to be unobtrusive about it, but exuded an aura of flattening negativity, sitting like a pasha in his armchair, his eyes shaded by an absurd green eyeshade while he read or played endless games of chess with himself and bossed my aunt around. Spinsters of the world, take heart. Your lot is a thousand times preferable to marriage with such a man. My aunt never expressed herself in words on the subject, but her chronic dishevelled exhaustion spoke volumes. She had produced two sons at this late age and, without even a token gesture of help from her husband, was bringing them up in the truest ethos of permissiveness. Which meant that the little fiends had her running up and downstairs, or round in harassed circles, the livelong day.

Perhaps, after all, she had a taste for martyrdom. But my heart was always squeezed by the sight of her weary face with the hair bundled anyhow into a knot at her neck that was always slipping, and her tiny misshapen feet with their painful bulging bunyons in worn canvas shoes, which were all that she could bear to wear. From her appearance one would never guess that her husband was earning a handsome salary, handsome enough to run a large car and own a substantial house in one of London's more desirable suburbs. Poor Aunt Caroline looked like her own char—except for that brilliant sweet smile of hers, which lit up so unexpectedly the defeated wreckage of her face.

Uncle Cyril was unsociable in the extreme. He even brought his portable chessboard to meals. But his presence, veiled by that absurd eyeshade, brooded over the proceedings. 'Pass the butter,' he would say irritably, cutting into the middle of our conversation. Or 'Carrie dear, make those boys keep quiet.' Every now and then he would lurch into his duties as host. 'Have some more,' he would say urgently to me, 'there's plenty more outside.' And immediately turn back to his chess game. Whatever it was—butter, bananas, meat, dates, oranges (for Uncle Cyril's table always bore quantities of things rare to obtain) there was always apparently, 'plenty more outside'. His version of fulfilment, expressed once in an unguarded moment when he had come back a little tipsy from a wedding reception, was a well-filled stomach and a well-filled purse. Under such conditions, he pronounced, a man could take mental enjoyment from the world around him without the heights and depths of emotional experience. 'I was so fascinated watching him become animated for once,' I recorded afterwards, 'that I didn't contradict him as I would other people.' On a previous occasion I'd drawn a blank asking him for his ideas 'about something, I can't remember what it was. . . . He said: ''No—I might have had twenty years ago, but now I'm just hedged around with figures, figures.'' (He was an actuary.) I felt very sorry for him when I heard that,' I wrote, 'but having a vicious temperament and never having gone through any ordeal I felt he shouldn't have *let* figures hedge him round and forget all about the lovely things outside'.

Whether Cyril had gone through any ordeal either, I don't know. But he certainly knew how to put others through them. Years after the period of my London visits, he bought a large country house somewhere in the home counties and transported his wife and sons to rattle round this mansion in isolated discomfort. Domestic help on a sufficient scale being unobtainable or too costly, my aunt's serfdom was extended from a five-bedroomed villa to the echoing spaces of obsolete grandeur. She confided later to my mother that for the first six months she staged a rebellion—but finally gave in. Later still, she got ill with cancer. It was found on the operating table to be beyond surgery. But her husband, never having learned how to take no for an answer, refused to accept the verdict. For once his authority was overruled and she finally had the last and dreadful word by dying in great pain. I'm quite sure that it is to Uncle Cyril that I owe my gut-level feminism.

There was nothing feminist, however, in my reactions to my new ballet teacher, Stanislas Idzikowski, with whom I fell instantly and slavishly in love. Idzi, as he was always called, had been a soloist with the Diaghilev Ballet. The *Encyclopaedia of Dance and Ballet* describes him as 'a very tiny dancer with prodigious elevation and technique, more suited to demi-caractere roles . . . than for romantic ones'. Nevertheless, he danced many of Nijinsky's famous roles including *Spectre de la Rose.* Tiny he may have been, but every square inch of him bristled with aggressive energy, and he had the blinding charm (when he so chose) of very gifted, very outrageous people. I never knew much about his relations with the ballet establishment, but I have a hazy impression that his difficult temperament may have put him outside the more honourable positions for ageing stars, such as ballet master or master-class teacher.

When I went to study with him he had his own studio, a sordid, cramped single room off the Charing Cross Road, where he presided in the company of Madame Evina (Madame Evie, to us), his 'devoted pianist' (see the above-mentioned Encyclopaedia). Behind her devotion hangs a tale. It was common knowledge that Maestro operated a *menage à trois*. Madame Evie had been his mistress for many years—she was a member of the *corps-de-ballet* in the same Diaghilev company. But it didn't prevent him from marrying a comfortable, billowy white-haired English woman, at which Madame Evie cut up rough and insisted on her 'rights'. With grim persistence she held on to Idzi, wife or no wife, and whatever compromises she had to make in life outside the studio, within its four dingy walls her reign was absolute.

Sitting brooding at her piano as though it were some laboratory for the distillation of magic essences, she had the quivering dignity of a permanently outraged duchess. She was touchy, jealous, affected, pitiful, not young. Yet one had to admit that she had both guts and a sort of crazed charm. Life force was not lacking. And in spite of the incredible garments she wore, the incredible scenes she could throw, and the affected silliness of her behaviour, there was a kind of naïvety about her and a gallantry in the face of adversity that made even a sharp-eyed little character-collector like myself feel vaguely protective. Only one thing I couldn't forgive her. She was the very worst pianist I have ever heard, and her most bizarre aberration was to believe that she was profoundly in touch with inspirational music.

My days were divided between class at Idzi's, sometimes preceded by a private lesson, and the hostel where I found myself in the afternoons listening in on the academic classes for the student teachers, which took place in a kind of tutorial form in the large living-room. My attendance was quite unofficial, but the English teacher, a characterful woman with a teaching method splendidly provocative of discussion, seemed glad enough that I should take part if I wished. I'm afraid I defaulted on written assignments, although, drawn still to some kind of thinking activity, my curiosity had been roused by her unorthodox ideas. She seemed to teach a variety of subjects, history of education, English, a little psychology, and I wish I had persevered with her work, for Mrs Truman gave a healthy jolt to my mental complacency. 'She makes me doubt whether I am as intelligent as I have been led to believe' I wrote in my journal—a salutary doubt to have planted from time to time, especially if the atmosphere is open and democratic. She was the first person I had encountered for a long time against whom I had to argue my disagreement cogently, the first person to disturb the alarmingly rigid ideas I was developing on matters of literary style, the composition of the psyche, and, in general, the laws by which human beings conducted their affairs. I could have done with a few more such provocative influences; it might have helped to break the confinement of a world view constructed largely in discussion with myself.

I also had a weekly French lesson with a faded, elderly French spinster who contrived, nevertheless, to make Molière fairly lively fare, and once a week there was an art class for RAD scholars — dance students who had been awarded a free ballet class and art class, of which I had been one for some years. To my astonishment, Miss Prentice, who taught us stage design, was so intrigued by my costume design for an angel in a mediaeval mystery play that she asked me to reverse it and draw the back view as homework for the next lesson. Flattered but irritated, I had to unscramble my elaborate arrangement of draperies and, worst of all, come to some decision about how an angel's wings fitted onto its back. As an exercise in fanciful anatomy it is to be recommended.

Several evenings a week were taken up by the Production Club, held at the Royal Academy of Dancing, where young dancers and young choreographers tried their paces. There was no choice about attending. If you were asked to go to the Production Club, you went. I did, with subdued cursings. The sociability of the hostel, particularly with the example of girls who could clock off in the evenings (the teaching students far outnumbered the performing dancers) in front of me, was already causing a stir of inner protest long absent in Edinburgh. Besides that, there was the fact that I was a newcomer and a stranger and that I was back in the corps-de-ballet, all of which removed any allure from evening rehearsals.

A further commitment was to be involved along with two other RAD scholars in Arnold Haskell's lecture-demonstrations scattered round Greater London. I have no idea who our audiences were, probably evening class attenders for dance appreciation, but we had to get ourselves up in full rig of tutu and flesh-coloured tights and demonstrate the different ballet steps as he talked about them. All went well initially, until a series of evenings when we worked carelessly—bored out of our minds at dragging out to these events—and came in for a sharp reprimand. I was given a strange exemption, being told that I was now 'professional' enough that even when I worked badly I could carry it off. For Haskell was still showing interest in me and giving warm words of encouragement when he came to watch our Saturday morning Scholars' classes. But it was at these classes, taught by Molly Radcliffe, a severe, feline lady, that signs of strain in my back were first commented on, the result of those misguided efforts on my part to achieve suppleness before strength.

It is clear from my own jottings that, despite my still urgent passion to be a dancer, I identified far more strongly with the teacher trainees, combining ballet with straight education, than I did with the professional dancers. The latter were, I fully recognised, far more glamorous, coming in late from Covent Garden or Sadlers Wells with their fashionable 'new-look' ankle-length skirts, their weary white faces reduced to painted lips and eyes, for even for the street their make-up had a degree of theatrical exaggeration, their knobbly arched feet stretched in exhaustion on the living room sofas. Of course they were the real thing. But if one wanted talk — well, there was no comparison. They talked shop, endlessly, all names and no sparkle. Whereas with the others, we talked and talked about anything and everything, simply for fun, and as the time wore on the conversation would turn to 'religion and the infinite and a bit of sex' (journal quotation) and we would feel that we were on the brink of unlocking the key mysteries, and finally stagger off to our respective beds bemused but certain we were on the track of momentous matters. I tasted, fatally, the enormous straightforward fun of being a 'normal' young girl among a group of other such normal young girls. They didn't have the ominous excitement of a dedicated career in front of them. They could look forward to social life, boy friends, marriage—some of the older ones already had fiancés. It was not that I consciously saw myself as being inevitably deprived of all those, but—there was always the Task, of self-improvement in body (dance) and soul (dance, and something to do with God) which meant that one was on a sort of constant vigil while others could come and go, sleep and laugh, and treat time as their servant. Deep inside I had a wistful feeling that life itself was too good and enjoyable to be relegated to something glimpsed out of the corner of the eye between pliés and self-castigation.

I was very, very happy during my first term in London, much of it coming undoubtedly from the fact that I was working at a new level, making progress. Idzikowski took great pains teaching me, and there was encouragement coming from Haskell and the RAD teachers. I was, on the whole, popular at the hostel and starting (slowly) to learn a thing or two about quelling the sharper juttings of individualism in the interests of good relations. The fact that I had almost no male company bothered me not at all, and a glimpse of one of my family (I occasionally went to Oxford to visit my brother now in his first year) was as ever delightful. When my father appeared for a three-day visit to London, I was overjoyed, except that, naturally, he wanted to watch me at class, an ordeal almost as bad as an audition.

However, he seemed pleased with what he saw and after that I could revel in the unaccustomed luxury of being lunched in a West End restaurant. Afterwards he bought me, extravagantly, an expensive spray in a florist's and pinned it to the lapel of my suit. I have a feeling that he was a little in love with me at the time, and that leavening his civil service trip to London by wining and dining his dancing daughter was a pleasant break in his averagely monotonous life. In the florist's at the same time as ourselves was a couple which attracted my attention. They were not young and not beautiful, but over the moon with a happiness impossible to conceal, and somehow this transforming joy on two very homely people spread a glow of shared humanity which made the occasion special for all of us.

Idzi's studio brought me in touch with a few interesting people and a few more very dull ones. His classes were on the whole not large, though occasionally attended by Big Names, more often male than female. I learned later that he was reckoned to be a better teacher of men than women dancers, but during my first term not a whisper of inward criticism did I raise. The day was made or marred by the amount of attention he paid to my work in class. Even adverse criticism was better, far better, than being ignored. At private lessons and *adage* classes where he often partnered me himself, he worked me very hard and afterwards Madame Evie would pat my hot cheek with her hard unsympathetic little hand and give her gracious judgment on my progress.

There was only one aspect of Maestro's character which I found objectionable. His arrogance and exhibitionism, dazzling bits of demonstration when he leapt and twinkled in the air, clad as he was in suit and brightly polished street shoes, were fine—all part of the show, the business of astonishing the bourgeoisie of us class rankers. But he had a vicious temper which he channelled almost exclusively in the direction of one unfortunate girl who, with the most dreadful dog-like devotion and absolutely no reward, came day after day to attend classes. I was amazed that someone so desperately untalented should have been allowed to take part, choosing to ignore the fact that dance teachers are there for business and not for the purpose of weeding out the unmentionables. Sarah was a sort of anti-dancer, her only gift that of performing a movement with a jerky disjointed gracelessness which would have been hard to imitate. I think it was her glum spiritless face as much as her amazing all-wrongness of movement that so incensed Maestro. And although I was genuinely shocked at someone so defenceless receiving such a constant barrage of mockery and insults—when Maestro likened her arabesque to a dog peeing at a lamp-post it was a sign that he was feeling mild and jocular—worst of all, I knew that by the laws of interpersonal dynamics Sarah was mutely *asking* to be kicked and kicked again.

The studio was not a sociable place. We came and went and were largely uninterested in each other except in a spirit of anxious competition during class. But for a while I made friends with a lively Balinese family, two brothers and a sister, all professional performers of their own dance form. I couldn't think why they were trying to train for ballet. I felt that to fit their own lovely way of moving into the rectilinear setness of ballet was a kind of desecration, like forcing some wonderfully shapely plant into an unsuitably formal frame. One of Tamara's brothers was amazingly handsome, and boringly aware of it. The other was homelier and much more human and amusing. (There is a strong correlation between masculine beauty and humourlessness—perhaps the same can be said of women.) Tamara herself, the youngest, had an exquisite body but a plain droll face, with something of her Dutch ancestry as well as broad eastern flatness in her features. After we had spent some contented afternoons wandering round the British Museum together, she asked me to come to a dance gala where she and her brothers were dancing. When I got there, with my mother who was in London, we were amazed to find ourselves at a red reunion with fervent communist speakers, including Kurt Jooss, taking the platform and shaming us into contributing to funds for the liberation of the Dutch colonies. Stiff and uncomfortable, for there is nothing more embarrassing than to feel politically out of key with a gathering, we waited for the performance to begin. In it I saw my everyday class companions transformed into mythical deities, and the contained voluptuousness of eastern dancing sucked me once again under its spell. Where this trio went when they left the studio I have no idea, but I missed them. Like all the committed communists I have known as everyday companions, they were merry and lively and as far from the stereotype of the faceless slave of dogma as it was possible to be.

Roads Taken and Not Taken

My second term started, after the Christmas holidays and a brief repeat of terrible homesickness when I got back to Fairfield, with no inkling of the drama which was to blow up within weeks of resuming my normal busy routine. It began with nothing more than a faint worry on my part that my right foot was getting increasingly painful when I did point-work. Minor injuries to joints and muscles were common enough, and I'd been laid off class a few times as a student with strains and wrenches. However, the persistent trouble in my foot made me decide to consult medical opinion, and accordingly I attended the clinic of a leading orthopaedic surgeon in one of the big London hospitals, who looked non-committally at my feet and said that X-rays would be needed before he could make an assessment.

A short while later, carrying my envelope of plates, I returned to see him, this time by private appointment at his consulting rooms, accompanied *in loco parentis* by the gruff warden of Fairfield hostel. The consultation was of the briefest. The great doctor scanned the X-rays and said brusquely without even bothering to look up: 'Yes, well, of course, if you persist in dancing you'll be lame for life.' In agonised disbelief I heard him explaining that because of the unequal length of my big toes and second toes, the first being longer than the second, the big toe was bound to bear the full burden of weight when I was on point, putting a strain on the joint that would cause it to collapse. This, on the right foot, was already starting to take place. That being said, we were shown out.

Even stiff-upper-lip ex-WRNS officer Miss Whiteley confessed later that her breath had been taken away by the incredible abruptness of this revelation. As for myself, I remember nothing except being shoved hastily into a taxi, the world, to use a cliché, in ruins around me. There must have been 'phone calls home, some kind of care taken of me, for I was in a state of shock. Never for one minute had I thought there was anything seriously wrong with my foot. Apart from the crushing disaster of being told, in so many words, that dancing was over, was the horrible feeling of bodily betrayal, like finding a friend turned traitor. My feet were all-important. One of them (and ultimately both, if the doctor was to be believed) was already an unsafe element. It was like finding some form of sinister rot in the foundations.

Factual memory takes up again at a kind of case conference that was held in the flat of Miss Kathleen Gordon (then director of the Royal Academy of Dancing) perched high up in one corner of Fairfield Lodge. I had never been up to these elevated quarters before, for there had never been any reason. Now, even in this bizarre situation, where I was suddenly the centre of compassionate attention, I still noticed wryly the contrast between the subdued luxury of this flat and our threadbare existence two floors below.

My mother was there (my father followed later, I think, but that too is unclear). She had arrived in a state bordering on breakdown, having wept all the way down on the night train from Edinburgh to London, in such a state of despair that she had had to pour out the whole tragic story to her companions in the third class sleeper. I felt desperate for her, embarrassed too, at this geyser gush of grief. And frightened. It was suddenly borne in on me how desperately she was involved with my life, how unhappy she must be at some level with her own—nothing I could make explicit to myself, just the clawings of unease. Who was supporting whom? Whose disaster was this?

Besides my mother, there was Miss Gordon, Miss Whiteley, Arnold Haskell, and Idzikowski, who kissed me warmly and full of concern. 'She has a very great talent,' he whispered tragically to my mother. 'Have some sherry,' cut in Miss Gordon in her clinical upper-class voice, that brand-mark of containment which through every vicissitude of public and private life retains its cool distancing edge. I sat on the edge of a chaise longue upholstered in some soft grey velvety material and sipped sherry several degrees too dry for pleasure. I'd lost the place slightly, not sure why we were all convoked, except that it was to do with me and my future. I felt important, bewildered, and also more than half disembodied, a little like a conscious corpse at its own obsequies.

It was Arnold Haskell who introduced a note of realism into the situation, one that I was unfortunately too shell-shocked to take in its full impact. At some point I was left alone with him, and he gave me a little talk, the burden of which was this. 'You are a lucky girl, Una,' he said. 'You have a fine intelligence and unlike many girls who go into ballet you can easily go back to studying and get into university. There are all sorts of openings before you. Besides,' he added, delivering the punchline, 'you would never become a second Fonteyn—and you know it'. There was a long pause while I tried to digest this known but undeclared truth. 'And for you, it has to be the first-class thing, or nothing. You want excellence.' He had got it in one. I did want excellence. In dancing—and he was really only telling me what I already suspected but didn't want to face—I did not have the capacity.

It was a conversation that was too brief and too one-sided. I was too much in awe of him and too bruised to find the courage to ask him if his words of praise since I'd come to London meant nothing? I'd also like to know, for my own satisfaction, whether he had given the matter thought, or whether he was talking off the top of his head. Whether he was deliberately trying to help me make a clean break, or whether, like that orthopaedic surgeon, he was coldly delivering himself of a professional judgment without much concern for the human consequences. I found his eagerness to see me on my way out of ballet almost as jarring as the verdict on my foot. Not that he had done anything so silly as string me along with inflated hopes. But he had shown marked interest in my work, and although I was a glutton for praise, I was also too anxious easily to accept as solid praise anything that didn't ring fairly true, and I had trusted as well as valued his encouragement. But I think at that point what I resented most was not so much his blunt common sense about my likelihood of reaching stardom but the idea that I could simply discard ballet and switch into some other pursuit, and that therefore I was 'lucky'. As if heartbreak didn't count. I have never been very good at responding to bracing treatment, at least in the first instance.

The next few weeks are so totally confused that I can remember little except my surprise that with this sudden upheaval in my life it still went on, in patches pleasantly enough. No one seemed certain what was to happen. I stayed on at Fairfield, attending occasional classes but doing no point work. I spent a lot of time with the other girls, forgetting for whole evenings at a time that my life was 'ruined' in the routine fun of hostel life, going to films, brewing up hot drinks and gossiping. Yet every now and then I would sit feeling that my existence had come unstrung, and was lying in my lap like a lot of rattling beads. It seemed tolerable enough in a queer empty way, although every now and then I would weep in a corner about it, but the idea that it could ever have the vibrant feel of purpose again was unbelievable.

Meanwhile, the idea grew that I should get a second opinion about my feet—from my parents, or Marjorie Middleton, Idzi, or my father's medical friend Frank, I do not know. Meanwhile, also, I had put Arnold Haskell's wise and significant words into a far corner of my mind. In the middle of the current drama, full of the theme of the menaced heroine, it was too complex a piece of humiliation to introduce the banal possibility that perhaps she wasn't worth the bother of saving.

In any case, I too was caught up in it and longed to have the verdict on my feet reversed. When a second consultant declared that my feet were perfectly strong, I joined with my parents in a day of rejoicing and celebration eating, after which they got on a train back to Edinburgh and I returned to Fairfield. But the day ended on a leaden note. Coming back with the joyous news that I was in the clear I met Miss Gordon on the stairs. It was nearly dusk and I could not see her clearly, but blurted out the glad tidings that I could go on dancing without fear of damaging my feet, another doctor had said so. She paused for a moment, obviously taken aback, and then her faint cold voice came through the gloom. '*Well,* my dear, I'm sure that's very nice for you.' And instantly my spirits flattened. She wasn't overjoyed. They didn't want me back. They'd all assumed that what had happened was unfortunate, but nevertheless a timely opportunity for a nice young girl to get back to ordinary life, and considering she was rather bright, wasn't it just as well?

To be fair, I imagine that Miss Gordon's non-committal caution was in part sheer surprise that something probably considered a *fait accompli* was being put into reverse. But set against the Wagnerian scale of my mother's emotions, and the Slav theatricality of Idzi's reactions, this tepid English response was the quintessence of subtle rejection. If I'd had any life-preserving sense I'd have looked for some sane, approachable adult and tried to examine the dire doubts about the whole business this encounter sparked off. I did, in fact, tell my mother something of my dismay over the meeting with Miss Gordon, for she wrote to her, and a reply came back in which Miss Gordon said that she was 'more than delighted' to hear the news. So perhaps the incident revealed more about *my* state of uncertainty for all my desire to be dancing again, than anyone else's.

It is certainly from then on that I feel I dragged part of myself unwillingly and unconfidently along the ballet route, unable to face the consequences of giving up and hoping desperately that the still existing infatuation for its particular beauty meant I had done the right thing. I don't know exactly what it was about the incident over my foot that was so shattering. Part of it was to do with the fact that I knew I had balked an important issue. I could not face the threat of becoming ordinary, of putting aside my tutu and tights and point shoes and facing the world as a lay member, with the humiliation of a sort of defrocking behind me. The role of semi-sacrificial 'dedicated' heroine was something that I had grown up with for the past several years, and my relationship with both my parents, particularly my mother, was strongly coloured by it. Nor could I face, squarely, the loss of my own particular fantasy of stardom. It was gone and I knew it in my heart, but, like trying to continue a dream that is fading at daylight, I went on with a forced, stale feeling, refusing to wake completely and say 'It's over'.

I felt devalued at every level, not least by myself. Nobody seemed to care what happened to me, the person. The doctor whom I first consulted could not have cared less that he was delivering a body-blow. My mother's uncontrollable distress was primarily to do with her needs, not mine, and—far too complex a consideration to grasp fully—I nevertheless sensed this and the threat of having her devotion withdrawn. That it might be a conditional thing had never occurred to me before.

Perhaps the only person who did give a little thought to the question of what mattered for me as a person, and not simply as an extension of my own or others' fantasies, was Arnold Haskell. For which, belatedly, I record my appreciation.

I don't think I made a decision to continue as a dancer, I gave in to indecision and a fatalistic feeling that I did not know how to stop, to turn back. The flow of events took me down the wrong turning, and led eventually into a very sticky quagmire, although the way remained thronged and lively and beguiling for some time to come.

The Shallows of True Love

The trouble with my foot flared up some time early in the year. Significantly, I did not write a word about it in my journal which was untouched from the end of January until mid-May, when I was back in Edinburgh on holiday. I started it up again with a feeling of need to try and put myself 'in touch' again. A kind of blight of spontaneity seemed to have taken place. Dancing was an effortful and burdensome thing, the result of that unresolved doubt about why I was still doing it, and a very real fear, in spite of the second diagnosis, about whether my feet would hold out. For a dancer, this is a fundamental threat, and the fairly lasting dent it made in my psyche is expressed in a recurrent dream which until recently presented itself whenever there was some ordeal, real or imagined, to be faced. The dream was always of being forced to dance on point with shoes that were either too hard or too soft, with a sense of acute dread because my feet were too weak to support me. It sounds mild as worry dreams go, but the threat of having to perform with this basic inadequacy was of the same cold-sweat quality as the fear of falling over cliffs, or motoring without headlights, or other catastrophic situations created by the unconscious.

I had lost faith in my feet, and I had drastically lost faith in myself. I had also failed to win a Royal Academy bursary for which I had been tipped as the favourite. 'I have never before reached such a rock-bottom,' I wrote during that spring holiday. 'Always a tiny store of secret confidence remained, in the fact that I had potentialities but only I could see them. Now my ideas have changed and I am not so pleased with I. That is the root of the whole trouble.'

The Shallows of True Love

To be questioning and uncertain of self and identity was of course a perfectly natural part of adolescence, but for me it had been held back, as I think it is for many people in narrow specialised situations, by the fact that problems were repetitive and concerned very clearly with practical issues of craft, rather than relationships. I'm told that nowadays 'even dancers', as one artistic director of a company put it, are more in touch with the world around them. The television screen and the general relaxation on censorship, as compared to the immediate post-war years, does bring other lives and other realities, even in distorted form, that much nearer. The debunking of strict authoritarian disciplines has something to do with it as well. I see dance teachers shaking their heads sadly at the poor calibre of effort that young dancers bring to their classwork now. Gone that iron edge of striving, the blind obedience to the notion of military-style perfection. It makes for rough and ragged ensemble work, which is bad for spectacle, but is a symptom of questioning which has its very positive aspects.

The reprieve over my feet, when it came, was not the soul-sweetener it should have been. I dragged my doubts day after day through classes where my work fell off noticeably, and I became more and more critical and questioning of the methods of once-adored Idzi. Things had gone remarkably sour. It was in this state that I found myself home for the Easter holidays, where I was to stay for several weeks in some kind of semi-convalescence, I suppose. I went back to the old studio to keep up training, made contact with various old school and studio friends, and, ripe for new and troubling emotions, fell in love.

Just to ensure the maximum of conflict and complication, the boy happened to be the younger brother of my current admirer. In such situations the laws of primogeniture, bred into us unawares by the rigid Presbyterian patriarchy which pervaded (and still pervades) Scottish education and family life, held remarkably firm. Malcolm and I knew we were in the wrong, breaking taboos, offending tribal custom. I was not his woman, I belonged, officially, to his elder brother Roderick. Built in,

109

therefore, was a measure of secrecy and threat which, it hardly needs to be said, added that touch of delicious burning acid to a situation already pulsing with intensity.

Roderick and Malcolm were the sons of a formidably ambitious mother and a gentle reflective father. They were brought up tough and aspiring and rigid, and since both were gifted and basically non-conformers, their own internal conflicts were acute. It is no coincidence that I appealed first to one, then the second, nor that I sniffed out kindred tormented souls caught between the burden of displaced aspirations from the older generation and the pressure of strong personal drives. The brothers were in a worse predicament than myself. At least I had found something which did in large measures reflect my own choice, however much the venture had got overlaid with other matters. But there they were, under compulsion to excel, although they were nowhere near the point of knowing their own particular direction. They were, particularly Roderick, all-rounders, with a combination of high energy and a diversity of talents that were out of the ordinary, though as far as one can judge these things neither of them was superlative in any one particular.

It is all too easy to see, after lives have gone rather bitterly astray, how certain combinations of needs and drives make the said lives virtually unliveable. Poor Malcolm, who several years after I first met him did in fact take his own life, once confessed that he swung perilously between states of such artistic megalomania that the problem was to decide whether to be a second Shakespeare or a second Dickens, and a sense of grovelling inadequacy when he knew with ghastly certainty that he would never be 'anybody'.

Roderick, a pioneer drop-out from university in the late 'forties when it was unheard of voluntarily to remove oneself from an unfinished degree course, dabbled in writing, acting, producing. Finally, his entrepreneurial drive triumphed and he set up a successful commercial film company. But his resentment and relentless energy remain, as does his cold disregard for human feelings —legacies of that pressurised boyhood in the dourest of all cities.

However much they shared in common problems, there was not a trace of physical resemblance. Roderick was, photogenically, the more beautiful. He was olive skinned, with glittering grey-hazel eyes, quivering flexed nostrils and a square taut face with full and rather cruel lips. His hand-clenched restlessness was one sign of a physical tension which I found almost unbearable. He was bright and sharp and teeming with ideas, all of which I liked as much as I was repelled by that sense of permanent smouldering protest in his physical being. We shared a lively mental life. We were going to choreograph a ballet together, for which purpose we started evolving a system of notation to write down the steps. We discussed, coldly and intellectually, poetry, prose-writing, art forms, his own plays, and, warily, the nature of human emotions. He accused me of being excessively cold and aloof, with some justification, for in spite of our excellent companionship, I withdrew sharply from something chillingly calculative about him.

Superficially, Malcolm had none of that. He had an engaging air of openness and casualness about him. His tensions and a similar calculative attitude were hidden under a fairly endearing physical typecasting—fair-haired, blue-eyed, six foot tall and pleasantly protective, athletic, of course, but not to boring obsessional proportions. Our relationship also took in culture, but that was an important frill on the central preoccupation of violent sexual attraction.

It was my first experience of the kind. The faint stirring occasioned by the episode with Jimmy were nothing compared to this. In any case, this was a boy, an animal at the same stage of tentative development as myself, not a man established in his physical adulthood, and therefore alien. The relationship was all the more upheaving because my adolescence had been so very pure, as much through lack of opportunity as by inclination, compared to the normal progression of fumbling experiments which even in the pre-swinging days took place. For several months it was high romance, the Real Thing. In Edinburgh we had snatched meetings, separated, like all young lovers with a taste for inbuilt anguish in their relationships, by barriers tangible and intangible. During term-time my Romeo had to dodge school regulations (he was a scholarship pupil at one of Edinburgh's few boarding schools) while at all times there was the need for vigilance on account of his elder brother. When I went back to London for a final few weeks some time in early summer I missed him painfully, and had my first taste of postman-watching, a pastime whose humiliations are never quite washed away even by the dizzy happiness of receiving the longed-for letter.

When I went back for the summer holidays, it was the classic cox-and-box situation. First Malcolm went to America on some kind of cultural exchange visit. So I resumed my relationship full time with Roderick—who, betrayed and angry, had no intention of ceding his rights as reigning monarch. Then he went to Italy, Malcolm came back, and we had our few weeks of idyll, struggling with lust and layers of clothing in wooded nooks or hollows on the hills outside the town, and discovering the fabulous erotic potential in the simple act of kissing. Then it was Festival time, and for the first week we went to everything we could, queuing happily for hours for the privilege of getting standing space for concerts and opera. It was my one and only taste of a 'holiday from life', the delicious switched-off dalliance that comes, with luck, when one is between one phase and the next. Then career matters intervened, for the Ballets des Champs Elysées arrived to take part in the Festival, and it seemed a heaven-sent opportunity to audition and try for a place with them. Love swiftly took a back seat and remained there for years, apart from a heavy leave-taking with both brothers (individually) just before I went over to France.

Les Ballets des Champs Elysées

Les Ballets des Champs Elysées was a company that had been started in 1945 by Roland Petit, and had grown out of performances at which young dancers and choreographers in rebellion against the orthodoxy of the Paris Opera Ballet had staged their works. This gathering of talent in design and dance caused such a stir at their first performance at the Theatre des Champs Elysées that the director, Roger Eudes, gave them the theatre as a home. Deeply involved with its work were Jean Cocteau, Boris Kochno, and Christian Bérard, former associates of Diaghilev, and the combination of their influence, the newly released choreographic talent, and some brilliant individual dancers like Babilée, Algaroff, Vyroubova, Jeanmaire and others, made it the brightest and most exciting company to emerge from post-war Europe. There was some reason to hope, with works like *Les Forains, Jeu de Cartes* and *Le Jeune Homme et La Mort* that ballet was emerging as a medium for ideas that fused intellect with drama, technical brilliance with creative vigour.

When it came to the Edinburgh Festival in 1949, the company was four years old. Petit had left to form his own group, the Ballets de Paris, but it still retained many of the original dancers on whom roles had been created, and had its customary dynamic impact on Festival audiences. In many ways it was a stimulating group to aspire to join, yet for a dancer as classically oriented as myself not necessarily ideal. However, then, as now, a chance to enter a company was rare, and when I stop to ask myself 'Why the Ballets des Champs Elysées?'—strongly encouraged by Arnold Haskell, once more taking an active part in my affairs, and also Marjorie Middleton, the most likely answer seems in terms of the job market, and the lucky break of being able to present for audition in Edinburgh where the place was not swarming with professional dancers.

My auditioning took the merciful form of attending company classes daily. The ballet master at the time, Victor Gsovsky, was a Russian, born and trained in Russia, and his eye still lit up with a watery gleam of enthusiasm at the sight of a nice classically trained dancer. The company, it seemed, could use one. Tall and gangling, with the alarming raw-meat complexion and premature shaky senility of the heavy drinker, he drafted me into the corps de ballet then and there, and wild with excitement I accompanied them down to London to take part in *La Sylphide* (first post-war production) and push plans for joining them in Paris later in the autumn, as proposed, a stage further.

I can only smile at my utter naïvety in taking literally all the lovely projects that were sketched out at that time. Arnold Haskell arranged a dinner with Irène Skorik, one of the company's ballerinas (whom I privately thought dull and insipid in spite of her long beautiful limbs and Haskell's admiration), myself and my father, during which we discussed the possibility that I should be her understudy in one or two ballets. Such ideas floated naturally and airily around, like the wreaths of after-dinner cigar smoke, as we sat and chatted over the remains of a bumper meal. I really believed that after that, it was all in hand, that I had only to turn up in Paris, and Skorik would take charge of the rest. In the event, I'm not even sure that she recognised me. By the time I actually joined the company, the gap in our relative positions, politely ignored when we had sat round the same dinner table as Haskell's guests, was so great that I did not dare raise the matter of understudying with her. In any case, she was embroiled with complicated intra-company politics, which was already simmering with unrest, though I did not know it.

What is stranger than my own absence of healthy cynicism was my father's. But—I cannot repeat too strongly—positively the worst mental preparation for anything to do with the theatre is the civil service. What one is and thrives on, the other is not and does not. Father had progressed throughout his life on the basis of solid endeavour and applying his mind to excellent effect within a known framework. The rules decreed that advancement came by those means. Pushing, shoving, string-pulling, knowing how to promote yourself or your dear ones by a bit of oversell—these were not the attitudes inculcated in senior public servants. Nor was the capacity to deal with fluid situations—and a ballet company, I soon discovered, was so fluid it tended to run out between your fingers. However, he did his best. Once in France, he was concerned to get a contract with a fixed duration out of the company management, instead of the 'three months and maybe more' open-ended situation which was being waved at us. The scene in which he confronted the administration degenerated, I'm afraid, into farce. Father's white hair started to rise in a sort of crest, lifted on currents of powerful frustration, as he wrestled with his own rudimentary French and the evasive urbanity of M. Robin, the company's administrator. In his excitement he slipped into Hindustani (a repeated tendency while he was in France) leaving the amazed M. Robin to raise eloquent French eyebrows, clearly wondering whether this respectable gentleman had suddenly taken leave of his senses. My mother clawed at his elbow trying to nudge him back to French, for the additional linguistic flourish was not clarifying matters. In the end we retired, baffled and uncertain what had been arranged, but it appeared to be a contract to work in Paris for a month, and then go on a four-month tour to Italy and Egypt.

France, land of the senses, entered my consciousness first through food—unbelievable, copious, exquisite food. I encountered it first on the train which carried us from Calais to Paris, my parents having decided to holiday for a fortnight and see me settled in—a huge celebration lunch at some unlikely time like three thirty in the afternoon, complete with wine and more courses than I had ever eaten at a sitting, with waiters dashing and swaying expertly, and conveying that amazing flavour of swift style which is the hallmark of the French.

115

It was the fanfare to a period of good eating which lasted till the joys of everlasting restaurant food (not, I may say, all at that standard of lavishness) started to pall, and more urgently, I had to face the alarming fact that for the first time since podgy little girlhood I was starting to put on weight. That, however, took several months. Meanwhile, starved not of necessities but luxuries during the war, and along with the rest of Britain, more resentfully during the post-war extension of rationing, I was in a state of permanent salivating greed. Never before had I seen such extravagant artistry applied to the worldly arts of food—and dress. The fabulous clothes shops round the Champs Elysées and the Faubourg St Honoré, both close to the hotel where I was based, not to mention the rococco abundance of the expensive patisseries, simply knocked me sideways. It was a whole new slant on life—pleasure, elaborated and refined and raised to an almost ecstatic height. Pleasure, the object of ingenuity and sophistication in its creation. I realised all of a sudden the essential shoddiness and contempt of standards which pervades British lifestyles across the class spectrum. And although I was basing my condemnation on wartime conditions, it was sound enough. The flood of material affluence, when it started to pour, did little to change the basic attitude of inelegance, ugliness, sloppiness.

Most of this pleasure-world was experienced, tantalisingly, from the wrong side of shop windows, particularly as regards clothes. From the start I was hard up, and continued that way only with variations in the direction of being broke, all the time I was in France, some two and a half years. I never managed to buy more than a few blouses, a couple of skirts, a serviceable jacket and a few odds and ends all the time I was there.

Although the Hotel Avenida, where we booked in, was right in the centre of Paris, nothing could have been more contrasted with the expensive quarter in which it was situated, nothing more safely, grayly petit bourgeois than its dingy shuttered facade, and its sparsely furnished inexpensive rooms. Its proprietor was a widow, black-clad and untalkative, and its sombre dining room was the one place in which we had a bad meal, a one-off experience which we did not repeat. But it was without doubt a place so rigorously *convenable* that my parents could leave me there without a tremor for my moral wellbeing. And, being within walking distance of the Theatre des Champs Elysées, it had its advantages. They were helpful, too, about storing my trunk when I went on tour. For an itinerant life with no home base, as I discovered, was shot through with recurring worries about how to dispose of one's possessions, how to connect up with them when necessary, how to make sure that mail did not go astray. Some of my mail was vital, like the parcels of point shoes which were sent over from Frederick Freid's in London, via my mother, for I soon discovered, to my dismay, that French point shoes were unwearable, and had to arrange for my own supplies.

I spent a month in Paris before going on my first tour, during which time I fell remarkably quickly into a sense of being at home in the place, despite language difficulties. Its novelty was not only unthreatening but heady, the antithesis of the attitude which comes upon the blasé traveller for whom the world has all been squeezed into a sameness of airports and modern hotels. I could not have been more acutely and delightedly aware of being in the Great Abroad, and of how different it was. On the erotic visual beauty of Paris it is not necessary to expand because anyone who has ever been there must have fallen for it. Yet the curious fact is that, after leaving it, which I did two and a half years later, I not only did not return for twenty five years, but blanked it out. It was not until I did go back, after all that time, for a brief few days' visit that I suddenly discovered that I was on totally familiar and much loved territory.

What of my re-encounter with the ballet company? The incident in which my father tried to put everything on a sound business footing was only the first of an endless series which all demonstrated one large dismaying fact. The company had no sound business footing. From the outset of my involvement with it there were serious financial problems. The first day that I turned up at the theatre, neatly dressed in a new cherry-red

winter coat (smart for Edinburgh, schoolgirlish for Paris) to
report to the management, I sat and waited and waited outside the
administration offices. Sitting next to me was Leslie Caron, then
one of the company principals, with fringe, ponytail, slanting
eyes, and the curious muddy pallor which marks out dancers and
quite unfairly suggests something unwashed about them. It is
nothing to do with lack of cleanliness and everything to do with
chronic fatigue, a totally indoor life, and the dulling effect of
perpetual greasepaint on the skin. Leslie sat there looking like a
Paris urchin in trousers and ragged shirt. I knew she talked a little
English, so I asked her why she was waiting. 'I need money,' she
said, 'to buy a skirt. There will be a reception after the first night
of the season, and I cannot go in trousers.' She added after a
pause: 'I do not know if they will give me any.'

Of the troubles of extorting money from the company I came to
be very knowledgeable, if not very successful. Like every dancer
who ever worked for them, I am still owed many months of
unpaid salary. There were times when we queued up to receive
1000 francs (about £1) and had to be thankful for it. But that was
later. During the first season, I did receive my salary, small
though it was, and the first tour was, by later standards, lavishly
paid. To my great disappointment, I had hardly any opportunities
to dance on stage during the Paris season, an otherwise magical
period. I also had the galling experience of seeing a cow-like
dancer being given opportunities that did not come my way,
because she was the wife of a male soloist who had been taken on
for the season, and part of the deal was that his talentless spouse
should get her chances too. It did not even occur to me to protest,
in spite of the fact that dressing-room gossip opined that I had
been unfairly passed over. I was lamentably slow at asserting
myself, meekly accepting the idea of serving an 'apprenticeship',
instead of getting out and doing battle.

Company classes and rehearsals were held at the top of the
theatre in an enormous room under the roof with the most
appalling floor, as hillocky as a field. The texture alternated
between hard and soft, as though in places someone had stuffed

straw under the lino. It was there that I started to get acquainted with the various members of the company. It was not large, and on the whole they were a friendly lot. The only other Briton was a male homosexual all too typically poncy and effete. We did not connect much. Apart from himself and an overweight character dancer (French) with legendary stinking feet, the rest of the men were vigorously heterosexual. There was the usual admixture of White Russians, men and women, and I soon learned that in the rating system, being Russian automatically pushed one up several notches. This was not really surprising. Mesdames Preobrajaenska and Egorova, ex-ballerinas of the Maryinsky Theatre, were still reigning supreme as teachers of the highest calibre, and there was a whole network of White Russian teachers and ballet masters and mistresses, which ensured that any dancer of that origin with any vestige of promise would have powerful backing.

The French girls ranged through the social scale from a member of the *haute bourgeoisie* (and very charming she was, without a smear of the forbidding snobbery that would have been part of the persona of her English equivalent) through petit bourgeois escapees, to uneducated little cookies from downtown *quartiers*. There was one witty raconteuse, half English, half French Jewish, who had become the company folkloriste, with a fund of vivid stories of past catastrophes and glories. Like so many articulate women, she had the sharpness of mind and tongue which earned her from time to time the epithet of *vieille fille*, in spite of her prettiness and vitality. She had a Brazilian fiancé who made infrequent visits to France, but some of the company men (your original male chauvinists) said unkindly it would do her good and shut her up to be ravished occasionally. 'But she has a fiancé,' I protested, as if vouching for the health of her libido. 'Yes, but he only ravishes her by airmail, and that doesn't really do the trick.'

As for my own libido, it was its resolute inactivity rather than its needs, that proved so complicated. In my relations with the men in the company, I made every blunder imaginable except actually to end up in bed with someone I didn't want. I didn't end up in bed with anybody for a long time, and though the great dead weight of Edinburgh disapproval, which still lurked in the background, and the thought of parental dismay had something to do with it, my abrupt confrontation with the sexual code of French manhood had rather more. I did not know that it was normal for men to go around in a state of permanent arousal, and that the mildest gesture of ceding—be it only an over-friendly smile—was taken as a signal for the hunt to be on. I didn't understand the first thing about the system of signalling between the sexes, nor the game of verbal fencing and provocation which could keep matters elusive and amusing rather than heavy and purposeful. It was the old awful trap of 'Let's be friends', as well as the fact that I had no inkling of my own normal sexual attractiveness. Previous romantic responses had been, so I thought (Malcolm notwithstanding), towards my 'finer qualities' and the fact that I had a pretty face. Body appeal, in itself, was something that did not form part of my self-image. I thought it was a rather lower-order kind of attraction. I wanted to stay cool and pure, but no one else did. Like every other nubile female in the company I was under strong pressure to be otherwise.

Matters became acute when we went on tour. To begin with I could not believe my ears. To have a commonplace conversation about the price of souvenirs taking place in the middle of a crowded shop suddenly interrupted by a *sotto voce* suggestion about retiring to bed with some rather lavish elaboration about the delights of my body was a situation which had at no point been prepared for in my education. I was aghast, embarrassed, and my stammering rejections had all the feel of some dreadful social gaffe, as if I'd tipped over my soup at a dinner party or been caught pilfering the petty cash.

Nor was the matter allowed to rest there. The usual sequence was persistent pestering and pressuring till I gave in to some fatal request like letting the pursuer come into my bedroom 'just for five minutes', I, still clinging with obstinate simple-mindedness to the idea that it was all in the spirit of cameraderie. But about getting into bed I was adamant. With some justification, I suppose, the offended man would then turn on the heavy reproach, and imply that I was a prick-tease, which, indeed, I was in my ignorance. He would be moody and churlish and catty. I was in some obscure kind of disgrace. All of which made me passingly unhappy, but left a lasting streak of resentment, if not actually man-hatred. My lack of readiness was apparently something shameful, and the very fact of being desirable and not delivering the goods made me feel like a trickster.

All this took time. To begin with there was not a cloud on the horizon, except for the scarcity of performing opportunities. Social life for the first month in Paris hardly included the ballet company at all, except to adjourn for aperitifs or coffee to the bar opposite the theatre after class or rehearsal. I had a modest whirl of gaiety, partly from introductions to one or two hospitable French families through friends of my parents, where I met young people who took me up, and partly through the excellent hospitality of Dr Donald Caskie, then president of the Caledonian Club.

Donald Caskie's story of wartime bravery in the French Resistance has been told in the *Tartan Pimpernel.* To my recollection he only once alluded to his experiences in an anecdote about being in the condemned cell waiting for the firing squad, and a more modest, approachable, unassuming man one couldn't hope to meet. Everyone, including himself, joked about his incurable, execrable Scottish accent when he spoke French in spite of years and years of exposure. Apart from his official functions as president, he went out of his way to put young Scots in touch with each other and with young French people by inviting us to rather sumptuous lunches at his flat. He also encouraged us to foregather for social evenings at the Club where we danced reels energetically, feeling the surge of national pride which tends to surface so much more clearly and easily when one is abroad. We also befriended each other with untypical warmth and enthusiasm, finding ourselves relaxed and outgoing—liberated perhaps—in the freewheeling atmosphere of Paris.

'My fellow countrymen are much more charming and friendly *à l'étranger* than in their own country' I wrote home to my parents. 'There are so many more people doing artistic careers in Paris, or rather, they are much more in the foreground.' I met aspiring singers, pianists studying at the Conservatoire, drifters doing vaguely literary things. But it was not only the ex-patriate Scots who foregathered under the banner of the Caledonian Club. It attracted various fervent Frenchmen, madly Scottophile to the point, in some cases, of claiming ancestry among Scottish clans. Maliciously we noted how they came in kilts and sporrans and hairy jackets, while the Scots boys came in trousers and shirts. One of my most persistent and embarrassing admirers was a stained-glass designer who solemnly declared himself to be eighth in line to the succession of the MacLeod chieftainship, and walked around self-consciously ennobled by a ghostly tartan halo.

As in London at Fairfield Lodge, part of me ached to be normal and remain in Paris to follow out the delirious sense of joyous novelty and discovery, like the rest of my compatriots. I envied the singing students who could stay put and study their art undisturbed. One of them, a girl from Edinburgh, became my firm friend—in Paris. If we tried to meet back home a blank shutter of reserve slammed down, as if we were defying each other to detect so much as a glimmer of our 'foreign' selves. Why this drastic cut-off, I don't know. It was not that we were privy to anything very salacious or offbeat about each others' lives, but there seemed to be a lack of guardedness in our relationship, over there, quite impossible to recapture in Edinburgh.

When the time came to leave on tour, I was heart sorry, having to turn my back on a pleasantly burgeoning social life, which included a charming young Frenchman whom I had met at the home of a hospitable family. Despite his Gallic poise, Henri seemed quite prepared to settle for friendship, if that was how I wanted it. Unlike the men in the company, he did not make me feel stuffy and prudish. Together we strolled round the tourist sights, ending up one windy afternoon along with one of his friends at the Eiffel Tower. To my astonishment, no sooner were

we settled at a table prepared to consume giant *babas au rhum*
than they asked me if I had a comb? Why I should find it so
convulsively funny to watch two young men attending to their
hairstyles in public I don't know. I suppose it was in contrast to
the grave self-conscious decorum which governed my family's
public behaviour. Indeed, one of the things I found hard to get
used to was the French habit of frank comment about personal
appearance. To have a spot on my chin examined with interest or
a critically appreciative remark made about the swing of my hips I
found equally difficult to take.

My nice new friend took me one night to the Folies Bergère,
where for the first time, I think, it occurred to me that my style of
dressing for best did not strike quite the right tone. My wardrobe
was sparse in any case and inspired by ideas of British niceness,
which meant that I usually wore a good wool dress with little flat-
heeled shoes—unless the occasion were really special when I
would put on my one and only party dress, a demure check taffeta
three-quarter-length with a low boat neck surrounded by a large
frill. It was always described as *très mignon,* but the wool dress,
soft grey, was not particularly *mignon.* It was just very
serviceable. Nevertheless, with a kind of uncertainty about how
to dress which I feel has dogged me most of my life, so that I am
never sure whether I shall turn up over or under-dressed for any
occasion, I graced the Folies Bergère in this irreproachable piece
of British utility couture. Gallant Henri gave no hint that
anything was out of place. On all sides there were French women
in chic little decolleté dresses—for it was a gala night, and the era
was that of the *robe de cocktail*—looking as naked and
consumeable as shrimp canapes. But he treated me with
immaculate attention, although the grey dress was not forbidding
enough to prevent him putting his arm round me and squeezing
me ardently as we watched plump, naked, much loved Josephine
Baker being hoisted to the summit of a human pyramid to roars of
applause.

I expect I was actually conforming to a known type. British
girls were almost inevitably the worst dressed and the best-

complexioned at any gathering. The French, of both sexes, never stopped raving about our beautiful skins. Apparently they even outshone the curious drudge quality of our clothes. But the only garment I possessed which aroused paroxysms of envy was a tartan skirt in sixteen gores cut on the cross, and tailor-made at R. & W. Forsyth. This apparently trumped all the natty little confections in mock-tartan which were displayed in every shop-window.

What was so enormously pleasant about the first few months was that I didn't mind my deficiencies. I couldn't but be aware that with regard to clothes the French girls were in a different league. Nor did I ever solve the mystery of how they managed to look so smart. Even the hardest up seemed to have a little local *couturière* who ran them up clothes of exquisite and individual cut. I knew my clothes were childish and unswinging, to borrow the vernacular of a later age, compared to theirs. It didn't seem to matter. There was still one law for me and one for them. For a while I was able to carry my old standards and values with me intact. If I seemed naïve and gauche by comparison, well, at home that way of behaving was perfectly acceptable. I hailed from a different culture. The discomforts of trying to merge the two had not yet started. On the contrary, my innocence and unfamiliarity with the ways of the world were, initially, a source of strong attraction. People seemed to warm to it, to find it refreshing.

I find it difficult to remember what role actual dancing was playing in my new Paris existence. It goes without saying that it was the background as well as the raison d'être for the whole venture. I was not in France for pleasure, nor primarily to receive either a broadening or a finishing to my education, whichever way one cares to formulate it, though I believe that the unquestioned benefits of being 'abroad', as my mother saw it, had also been a factor in entering a French company. I wasn't the first member of my family to taste Gallic culture. As soon as post-war travel opportunities and exchange visits had opened up my mother had sent my sister to spend the long summer vacation with a French family. Jill came home less than impressed. She did not find the experience of life on a fruit farm near Montaubon up-lifting. It had been exceedingly hard work and the scope of enter-tainment appeared to be confined to sitting en famille of an evening while Madame and her daughter knitted endlessly, the latter sit-ting with her feet soaking in a basin of hot water to ease the pains of a day's fruit-picking toil. She had struck exceeding unlucky — but no more so than many a hopeful au pair who found herself drudging away for a French family, as her French counterpart did in Britain. The great abroad had many ways of turning sour.

But I was in Paris to advance my ballet training, and however little I can remember in depth about my reactions to new teachers and classmates (the journal had been left behind, and for the next ten years or so I lost the habit of recording) I know it was the unquestioned underpinning to my existence there. I went to the Studios Wacker to attend classes, then and for many years the centre of ballet activity. It was an unsavoury crumbling warren of a place off the Place Pigalle, where ballet teachers famous and unknown, reputable and dubious, rented rooms of all shapes and sizes to cater for their following. High up in the building tiny aged Madame Praeobrajaenska, ex-ballerina of the Maryinsky, armed with a stick taller than herself to keep time, held her daily classes. I went there for a while, and Madame praised my work but scolded me for looking too serious. For a while I went to Madame Egorova, then moved to Madam Rousanne, elderly but with hair dyed a startling dense black, and one of the most popular teachers in Paris. She was so popular that barre-work became a question of the strictest timing, in order to avoid entangling one's legs with the dancer in front and behind. Space was a dreadful problem, and so was air. The place was suffocating and stank, as all dance studios do, of sweat. There were times when it was impossible to find space to carry out the movements properly. But Madame Rousanne was the Ballets des Champs Elysées' favoured teacher, and obeying some compulsive law of herd imitation, I continued to go there, although the odds against getting any individual attention were high, partly through weight of numbers, partly because the class was studded with stars.

125

Whether I was making progress or not, I really don't know. I worked immensely hard, as I always did. My foot seemed to have stopped giving acute trouble, but that forced, strained back complained from time to time. At company classes, under Gsovsky, I retained my position as one of his favourites. But my luck was out—as indeed it was throughout my time with the company. Had I but known it, I had hitched my wagon to a falling star, and although the true precariousness of the situation was concealed—at least to me—for the next few months, even I could see that what changes were taking place were not for the better. Gsovsky left the company, and was replaced by Marika Baesobrasova as ballet-mistress, a handsome, hard-faced domineering woman, now the head of a flourishing ballet school in Monaco. Despite her present international reputation, she was, in my view, a thoroughly mediocre teacher whose sole merit as a trainer was that she knew how to crack the whip. As far as I could make out, her interest in the company's productions came a very poor second to furthering her own various causes. At the same time tyrannical and slovenly, I believe that her appointment was a disaster for the company. She was a woman who went in for close favourites and hated outcasts. I was neither one nor the other; but I watched dancers she disliked crumbling under the lash of her tongue and an obsessional campaign of virulence, or withdrawing into indifferent shoddy work. I did not believe she had any real love of dancing.

Marika was, at that time, a thin, taut, arrogant beauty. According to the professional lechers of the company, she was ready to keel over into any pair of masculine arms at the slightest encouragement. This I cannot vouch for, as I did not keep a close watch on her behaviour; I only know that I was disgusted and incredulous when I met her official paramour, an elderly pot-bellied lawyer of considerable affluence. The idea of the slim young Russian woman coupled with this flabby dignitary I found quite revolting. Such arrangements between physically decaying men of substance and very attractive young women were not uncommon. A long-standing French custom was still vividly alive, and probably still is—doubtless a business arrangement which satisfied certain needs of both parties. Nevertheless, I found it outrageous—more, I simply didn't know how Marika could fulfil her part of the bargain.

My immediate prelude to setting off on tour with the company was the conclusion of some fearfully complicated pieces of official business regarding my status as wandering unaccompanied minor (under eighteen years of age). With the French authorities I had no problems. They seemed uninterested then in keeping tabs on foreigners juvenile or otherwise, working in their country. Officially, I was supposed to have both a *permis de séjour* (allowing me to stay in the country) and a *permis de travail,* authorising me to work there. I may have acquired the former, but I worked in France on and off for two and a half years without a work permit. It was the British authorities that took a keen interest in my activities. As a minor abroad on my own, I was not free to go to any place that had not been specified in advance and entered on an official document, stamped and approved. This requirement, given the Quixotic way in which the company's plans could change, gave me nightmares. Before going on tour I extorted a list of the towns in Italy and Egypt where we were to perform, and, equipped with the information, had to double back to London, where my father met me, down from Edinburgh for the purpose of signing various documents, along with myself. These officially sanctioned my presence in the specified places, and no others. I was to report to the British Consulate whenever I arrived in a new town, and the penalty for failing to comply with these regulations was a fine of £200—no mean sum in 1949—which my father had to guarantee to pay. At the time he was so hard up that he had to ask his friend Frank to agree to cover this, should the need arise.

Staggering under the responsibility for this vast sum, I used to break out in a cold sweat when a casual announcement on the company notice-board alerted us to the fact that we were taking in a couple of extra towns, or missing out one, during the tour—until, belatedly, I realised that what the British authorities didn't know they wouldn't grieve over, and that with a bit of fiddling with dates I could more or less make my itinerary match the one on the document. I also found that underworked consulates in foreign towns, particularly the smaller ones, took a much more casual view of things than the grim centres of officialdom back home. And informally, the contact with consulates sometimes turned out delightfully. In Florence, when I got there, the hospitable and knowledgeable wife of the consul took me all round that beautiful town, and asked me to spend Christmas with them, while the rest of the company hot-footed it back to France.

On Tour

Touring, of course, is largely trains, hotels, theatres, and more trains. I have a sort of composite picture of a compartment in a train somewhere in Italy, full of semi-soporific dancers. The only wakeful one would be Hélène Constantine, an American dancer with strong fundamentalist religious views, and the kind of acidulated sweetness of smile which frequently accompanies such beliefs. She had a tiny pallid dark-haired daughter who accompanied us on tour, and was under such severe discipline that even my illiberal heart (which regarded children as an unmitigated nuisance in most situations) bled for the little mite, struggling to learn to knit on the swaying train with her dragon of a mama losing patience over her mistakes. Hélène was married to Eddy Constantine, a crooner with a swarthy pock-marked face and horn-rims, who also materialised from time to time. But their marriage, I was told, was in difficulties, and they later divorced.

Propped eternally in a corner, it seems, was Nicky Polajaenko, American-Russian, dark, good-looking and perpetually sleepy, not only on trains. On stage, there was a faint lethargy about his performances, as though, knowing he was tall and had a good stage presence, there was no need to pull out all the stops and make himself uncomfortable. And as a partner, he had some idiosyncratic habits, like steadying his ballerina by putting his hand firmly over her outstretched foot in arabesque—something which should never be done unless she were in danger of taking a header into the orchestra pit.

Off stage, his sleepiness was like the smoulder of a big cat sunning itself. I liked Nicky, and he liked me, but unfortunately he was already in partnership with a dashing, exceedingly emancipated soloist who had commandeered the gullible young man and was in full liaison—which, I cannot help feeling, ran aground from time to time through boredom. Their grasp of each others' languages was slight, and Nicky seemed to be under permanent criticism, sometimes for being inattentive, sometimes for the opposite, at which Josette would say with a strong Americanised accent 'You are *bothering* me, Nicky—stop *bothering* me.' Nevertheless, she was firmly possessive, and firmly broke up any conversations with me that became too animated. One thing I did not forgive him—he took a photo of me in the train, fast asleep, with my mouth sagging open in the classic idiot-look, which I thought was a poor joke.

From time to time our torpor would be shattered by the approach of a main station. At Milan for example we had three minutes to get ourselves across to our connection at the far side of that vast terminus. There would be a stampede towards the piled up mountains of cases at the end of the corridor, a hysterical scrabbling, and a streaming trail of dancers running—one hoped in the right direction—across the station. Then back we would slump into a state of suspended animation until the upheaval of arriving at our destination.

If France had been the heady introduction to the idea of pleasure elevated to a fine art, Italy was where Art itself, both with a small and a capital A, really hit me between the eyes, except that such a lovely experience merits a less violent metaphor. We started our tour in the ancient town of Bologna, where to my amazement I found arcades, Romanesque churches, cloisters and bell towers, straight out of the pages of my father's books on architecture. It was like coming face to face with characters out of fiction, and as delightful. Why the architecture of northern Italy should have had this effect on me of a kind of magic of incarnation, I don't know. In Paris, father had taken me round the Isle de la Cité, Notre Dame, La Sainte Chapelle, St Julien le Pauvre. He'd shown me the curious lofty encounter between Gothic and classical styles which meet in St Eustache, all of which had impressed me without much effort, for my father had an inspired way of bringing achitecture to life. But the Italian thing was different, perhaps because I was seeing, not single pieces of fine or picturesque architecture, but whole clusters of buildings with a sense of organic connectedness, as if they were plants that had grown together.

It was in Florence that the combination of awe at being surrounded by Works of Art, and the first stirrings of conviction that it was entirely right and natural to be amongst buildings and objects as shapely and expressive as man can make them, fused into a sort of mild delirium. I found myself in a hotel flanked on one side by the church of St Maria Novella and on the other by Filippo Brunnelleschi's Foundling Hospital, whose slender and delicate arcade I had stared at often in my copy of Pevsner, for if there was one style I loved it was the early Renaissance. Here I was, quartered for a fortnight, literally on its doorstep. Still dazed by this sense of discovery—that all these creations actually existed outside the pages of books of appreciation—I found myself gazing at Michelangelo's David, at Benvenutuo Cellini's Perseus, at Donatello's Judith and Holofernes, at Ghiberti's Baptistry doors—in short at all those things at which tourists gawp with or without cameras. But this was 1949. Winter time. No tourists. And I was a seventeen-year-old semi-barbarian (in spite of the assiduous appreciation) responding for the first time in a completely spontaneous way to these towering celebrations of aesthetic vitality and superb craftsmanship.

Furthermore, it was the first time I had realised that the place for art is in the market place, to be passed and semi-ignored and ingested along with the rest of street life, as well as gazed at with concentration. Of seeing Botticelli's paintings dimly perceived beneath layers of dirt in the Uffizi Gallery, I have a far less emotional recollection, though the contents of the Bargiello, where the consul's wife and I wandered round in an icy chill, which the stones seemed to breathe out, must have played their part in seeding my interest in sculpture which surfaced decades later.

Most of these excursions I made by myself, but company life was sociable enough. We went off in threes and fours to eat; we exchanged tips about shopping, easily the most popular activity on tour, and accompanied each other to find ways of spending our money. In Italy, it was leather, gold and silk, that emptied our purses. I felt I had tasted the genuine flavour of luxurious acquisition the first time I bought hand embroidered silk shirts, and when I invested in a chain of gold links (which I had later to sell) I started to understand the appeal of collecting booty.

Spending on tour was actually an important matter, a sort of investment as well as a time for indulgence. It was the only time we had anything like real money in our hands. For living expenses were paid at quite a handsome rate, startlingly so, compared to the token salary that we were supposed to get (but seldom did) in Paris. It was a time to replenish wardrobes, acquire things that would be impossible to get otherwise. It was also the only time we could extort some portion of this never-paid salary, which was done by the following method. Having deliberately overspent our living allowance on food and purchases, we would go with our hotel bills to the administrator (individually, of course) and ask for money 'on account from my salary' to put towards the bill. There would follow a terrible scene with threats of being left behind 'as an example to the rest', to which the invariable response was 'All right, I'll stay.' Nobody was ever left behind. Nor, I think, did anyone push their luck too far in the matter of the sums demanded.

It was towards the end of our stay in Florence, which had been interrupted by a five-day break over Christmas, that I got ill, briefly but unforgettably, and entirely through my own fault. It was, in fact, a ghastly retributive experience for the sins of overeating. Not content with stuffing myself with pasta, prosciutto and cheeses ripe to the point of mobility, all washed down with the lovely local wines, I discovered a cafe where they served—my stomach still heaves at the thought—bowls brimful of slightly sweetened whipped cream. Disregarding the heavy meal I'd already eaten after the performance, I treated myself to a portion, rather to the amazement of my companions. Next morning, I knew that I was mortally ill—nothing but fast-approaching death could explain the abyssmal sense of nausea, and the conviction that I would never raise my head from the pillow again. I had to miss class and rehearsal, lying in neglected misery till one of the company came to enquire what had happened. I told her. She knew at once what was wrong. There are only two complaints in the French repertoire of everyday illnesses—a *crise de foie* (liver upset) and a *crise de nerfs* (something rather more transient than a nervous breakdown). It was clearly a severe case of the former, and in spite of the narrow basis of judgment, I knew she was right. My long-suffering liver had groaned aloud at last. Once I had recovered, it felt as though I had passed through some kind of initiation rite. I could now join in as a veteran when the conversation turned, as it frequently did, to matters of diet and health.

My room-mate for part of the Italian tour was a strange Dutch woman, called Tutti. It was considered hilarious that we roomed together—Una and Tutti—one and all. Tutti, although a slightly sybilline creature, was basically a good sort, a rough diamond, and an exemplar of the fact that, unlikely as it seems, in ballet one really does find all types. No longer very young, and living a life of borderline poverty in Paris, she had some of the characteristics of a religious fanatic as well as those of a foreign legionary. As she did her warm-up exercises in the wings before a performance, her eyes would be raised to some vision of the Virgin Mary somewhere in the flies, and at the end she would kiss a crucifix and genuflect. But her language was a rich barrackroom string of obscenities as soon as the slightest thing upset her. Every second sentence began with '*Merde alors!*' and not many people escaped for long without being addressed or referred to as 'stupid cunts'. She had restless delicate fingers, not fearfully clean, always plucking at something—her hair, often tied up in a bundly old scarf, her clothes, usually the fags which she smoked incessantly, producing a faint tanned smear round her mouth, which was also mobile and delicate. But strong in her features was the image of an archetypal Dutch old woman's face, part peasant, part witch, and in spite of her kind-heartedness I was slightly afraid of Tutti, whose temper could do unexpected things, and whose wrath, one felt, would in extreme instances resort to spells and destructive incantations. The broomstick, I felt, was never far out of sight, all of which is grossly unfair, for she was generous and warm, if also earthy and abrupt.

She also told intriguing and scurrilous stories about company members, past and present, but the saga that came round time and again concerned her own pure and unrequitted passion for Jean Babilée. Privately, I used to think that if my own feelings had been so seared the last thing I would want to do would be to tell everyone about it years after the event. But for Tutti it was all still alive (though I hope purged of its trauma) and, paradoxically, a matter for some kind of pride. As a dancer, she was immensely conscientious, and if only she hadn't had the most insensitive feet I have ever seen on a professional dancer, the rest could have been enjoyed.

When we went to Cairo, which we did after leaving Italy, I shared with Danielle Darmance, a very different lady. Danielle was an acrobat-dancer, slim beyond belief with a funny chic/ugly little face, and impeccable taste in clothes. She was a leading soloist, which meant that normally she and I did not find ourselves at the same restaurant tables. So how I came to share a room with her, I don't know. However, we landed up in the same airy *pension,* run by a Greek family with a son, handsome in the rectangular-headed Greek style, who was courteous and obliging and attentive. His mama and papa played much the same parental role for their pensionnaires, so, what with our enormous double room and all this family kindness, we had berthed satisfactorily. But I don't think it helped my sense of being in some mysterious way remote from the world in which the other girls operated to be told by the Green couple that I had the face of a *petite sainte.* I did not feel at all saint-like, only rather bewildered and slow in learning how to develop the necessary chic, slick coping behaviour of the others.

On Tour

Out of the goodness of her heart Danielle had constituted herself some kind of informal guardian to me for the duration of the Cairo visit, and it is certain that I needed some steering, for life in this cosmopolitan capital was more complex than during the Italian tour. It was almost the last year of Farouk's reign, and the big rich shops and hotels and restaurants told of a large and wealthy European population. The company had already performed in Egypt and was very popular. But I felt suddenly ill at ease in this curious atmosphere of fat wealth and jaded sophistication as I had not in Paris or Italy. My frame of reference was even less adequate to deal with what I encountered.

It was, in fact, when we got to Cairo that I started to feel the first effects of what must, for all its pleasures, have been a stressful few weeks since leaving home. I have always tended to get swamped by 'input', taking in impressions faster and more voraciously than I can assimilate them. And certainly the stream of new material had been non-stop, added to which I was learning a new language at a feverish rate. I found it keenly stimulating, and was always on the alert for new words, trying to piece out the meaning from the context of the conversation, and glad of that reasonably sound basis of school French and those bits of tuition that had been continued after leaving school. But in the event Molière and a sound grasp of syntax hadn't been enough even to help me buy a metro ticket. However, I had a good ear and an intense dislike of not being able to make myself understood, two valuable assets in learning a language at speed. By the time we got to Cairo, I was reasonably fluent, but my mind felt raw and throbbing with its overdrive activities.

The first evening was dismal. It was before the discovery, or rediscovery of the Greek pension. I found myself suddenly alone, deserted, in a strange hotel. All the other girls seemed to have friends and contacts from the previous visit and had rushed off to dine with them. It was the first time since I'd left home that I felt acutely and dejectedly lonely, spare, an outsider. There was nothing for it but to go to bed early, symbolising a kind of defeat, and there I snuffled myself to sleep in the grip of a bad spasm of self-pity. My emotions were not much lightened by a telegram from my father which I found waiting at the theatre the next day, a telegram which read like a furious reprimand for my failure to write home and let them know my movements. I was pierced to the heart by this grim message from my loving father, ending with the stern command: 'Write at once.' I'm not sure which was agitating him most—fears for my well-being or the threat of having to pay up that £200 should I deviate from the programme sanctioned by the British consular authorities. As I've already explained, this anxiety of innocent disobedience due to the vagaries of the company's plans hung constantly over me. Father's telegram sent me scuttling first to the British Consulate, then to buy stamps and inscribe a penitent letter home, the whole operation being copiously watered by tears, including the visit to the consulate, where a tactful young man (perhaps used to the sight of young female nationals in distress) ignored the fact that I sobbed my way through the official 'checking-in'.

That hump over, life picked up again. We did the sights; first, of course, the Pyramids at Geza and the Sphinx. My memories are not entirely clear, but I rather think the Sphinx was then somewhat drifted up with sand, so that the creature had an unexpected fireside look about it. What I do remember vividly is the gasping claustrophobia of crawling on hands and feet up a long interior corridor to get to the royal tomb (empty of course) at the heart of the Great Pyramid. The corridor was at a fairly steep gradient and not more than three feet high. Grunting my way along behind the rear quarters of an Arab guide I was acutely aware of the vast tonnage of stone on top of me, and mystified (I still am) as to why, with all the labour and ingenuity involved, they hadn't made a decent man-height approach. In fact, I still don't know how they got the royal corpse there unless it was placed on some kind of sledge.

Even more vividly I remember that some of us yielded to the pressures of one of the swarm of Arabs offering horse-rides, and that Nicky Polajaenko playfully decided to race me once we were fairly mounted and under way. Unfortunately his equestrian control was no better than mine, and both our horses simultaneously shook off the role of hired hack and played at being fiery Arab steeds for a few hair-raising minutes. I felt my mount gathering speed, his head suddenly becoming firm and obstinate as I sawed at the reins. 'Make for the open ground' yelled Nicky, as he plunged past, and I slewed round as best I could in the direction of a receding vista of sand. I was apparently about to be carried off into the desert, my hair streaming out and the wind fanning a hot flush of agitation. With the last remnants of common sense I noticed a small knoll coming into view on my left, tugged the horse's head round in its direction and the animal fortunately received the message (or decided the joke was over) and came to a stop, just like a bicycle losing momentum, at the top of this rise. When he caught up with us the Arab in charge scolded us both severely like naughty children and the rest of the ride was conducted at perambulator speed.

Cairo and Alexandria supplied the nearest thing to the glamorised version of theatrical life that I, at least, ever tasted. The theatre in Cairo, the opera house which had been inaugurated by the first performance of Verdi's *Aida,* was the most opulent I ever danced in. (It was burnt down about eight years ago.) Even the *corps-de-ballet* dressing room had the gilded look of star territory. There were still echoes of Verdi, pretty dreadful ones, sounding each night, for the then Egyptian national anthem was a little number he had scribbled down during rehearsals, so legend has it, and although there could be hot competition for the most ridiculous national anthem in the world, I would back that as a certain winner. We all used to giggle routinely waiting for the curtain to go up when this tin soldiers' tooting of sixteen bars' length—the maestro had not over-exerted himself—struck up.

I enjoyed dancing in Cairo for two reasons. Firstly, I enjoyed the grandeur of the setting and the sense of occasion. Secondly, I had more chances of performing, was dancing well, and was told so. Because of the large stage, and the fact that we were there for two weeks, the full repertoire was presented, which included ballets like *Les Amours de Jupiter, Coppélia,* Act II, and *L'Amour et son Amour* as well as the more easily transportable *Treize Danses, Les Forains, La Rencontre,* and others. My rather meagre opportunities of performing were stepped up accordingly, and as one of the other girls got ill I had also to take her place in various works. I knew I had acquitted myself well, and a sort of kindling of interest in my own potential—something I had not felt for a while—added its measure of excitement.

Offstage, we were fêted and dined and wined and taken to parties and receptions, and there seemed to be an endless supply of rich young men, often of mixed European and oriental parentage and mostly plump and dark-haired. I found them unappealing, and usually turned for protection to older men, a need for a father-figure often blinding me to the possibilities of much worse confusions. In Alexandria, I found myself the sole guest of a cadaverously distinguished Maltese gentleman with an enormous house, who entertained me very properly to lunch at which his elderly black-clad mother presided. One look at my usual school-girlish outfit of sensible neat jumper and woollen skirt (it was winter and quite chilly) must have made him realise that seduction would have taken on the qualities of child molestation, and indeed his behaviour was exemplary except that he tried to interest me in dancing with him in a low-lit corner of the salon from which mama had withdrawn. Nevertheless, I emerged with a feeling of relief. Once again, I had been out of my depth, in a situation I could only handle by withdrawal.

Yet the incident which earned me a startling tongue-lashing from Danielle was one, I am convinced, in which my trust in the man concerned was entirely justified. Through my friend Tutti, I had got to know one of the senior curators of the Cairo museum, an erudite and gentle man called, like every second Egyptian, Gamal. He had taken us into all sorts of corners of that vast cultural repository normally barred from the public. I wrote back to my parents proudly that I had seen the royal mummies 'which no one is allowed to see, not even the American Ambassador' (I'm not sure why I instanced him as the quintessence of the eminent who were debarred this privilege). I was impressed by the honour if not by the exhibits, which I found rather insignificant and pathetic. The only connection with live human beings was, grotesquely, the hair, and one negroid king with his frizzy curls still intact bothered me. More significant were some of the riches of Tutankhamun's tomb which, again, we were allowed to view privately, and which I could say with pride I had already seen when the exhibition came years later to London.

Gamal was very courteous and kind and correct, and when he asked me if I would be interested in seeing some belly dancing, I had no hesitations in following the promptings of curiosity and saying 'yes'. We went along one night after our own performance was over to a club where this activity took place. I was slightly taken aback at the fact that, apart from myself, there seemed to be an audience only of men. I also noted with surprise that my dignified Europeanised companion responded to the same reflex as all the other men, and when the plump girls on stage started oscillating their abdomens (choreographically all rather dull) leant forward with a loud throaty 'Ah-Ah' of approval, stretching out his hands as though he would have liked to grasp that heaving flesh. It was an impressive mass-reaction, that chorus of 'Ahs' and the forward thrust of bodies. In fact, the audience was markedly more interesting to watch than the stage-show. And in defence of my presence there, I may say that on this occasion I was not being simply naïve. As well as a lack of forward thinking, I had a genuine anthropological curiosity, and having done my duty by dead culture in the museum, saw this as an opportunity to do the same by the living.

But Danielle did not see it that way—not that I tried, or had the opportunity, to explain. When I got back to the pension that night, unmolested and unscathed, she, having heard from other company members where I'd been, was furious with a kind of tight-lipped disapproving fury which rocked me backwards. Danielle was no prude. She had men-friends, probably lovers, though she was discreet about her relationships. She had not batted an eyelid that I had been, with others from the company, to an all-night party at the flat of two wealthy brothers where we'd smoked hash (I handling the joint as if I feared it was going to explode into a cloud of demons), after which we'd gone on a jaunt into the desert where the car had broken down, and we had stood around for hours in the bitter wind while our stoned hosts tried to restart the vehicle. Yet with the Egyptian nightclub incident I had clearly overstepped some boundary between what was and was not done. 'Ça ne se fait absolument pas!' she kept saying severely, it was not the kind of behaviour expected of 'une jeune fille bien'. But what precisely was so 'not done' about it was never made clear. Was it a matter of going native? More likely, in view of the all-male audience, such spectacles were probably the equivalent of blue movie-shows—neither chic nor respectable to attend.

In spite of the novelties and excitements, I wasn't sorry when it was time to leave Egypt. I had found it a restless, noisy experience; added to which I was from time to time aware that I was on the defensive about being British. Since most of the inhabitants whom we met were likely to have affinities, if not actual blood ties, with France and French culture, and since much of the last hundred years of history in Egypt concerned the rivalries and enmities of British and French, my sense of anti-British feeling was probably well-founded. Being my father's daughter, and at that time light years away from taking a critical stance on Britain's imperial behaviour, I resented this. Flying back to Sicily, thence to continue our tour of Italy, had a quality of home-coming. Europe, I felt, was definitely my place.

Paris Time Two

At the end of March 1950, the company disbanded for a month's holiday, and I came back to Edinburgh. After the holiday there were to be two long tours, one to Australia, followed immediately by another to South America. I was taken aback at the idea of being so far from home for so long a time—nine months to a year—and also determined that if I went I should have opportunities to dance other than in the corps-de-ballet. I tackled Marika, the ballet-mistress, on the subject, and for what it was worth she assured me that I should have more and better things to do now that she knew what my work was like.

The last month of the tour had been spent in Cannes, a rather sleepy month, for whatever it is like out of season now, then it was very much in mothballs waiting for the summer and the holidaymakers. Nevertheless there were enough outrageously expensive clothes shops open to allow us to commit a few extravagances, and I acquired my first (and only) smart and typically French outfit, a dark blue two-piece ensemble with a sailor-top sweater and clinging accordeon-pleated skirt, very much *à la mode.* Clothes can do much, if not everything, for the personality. In that outfit I felt I had a new French sophistication, that I shed my air of *'petite étudiante',* as someone described me, that my figure benefited by material which clung to it rather than meeting it only at shoulders and waist.

My figure, however, was starting to cause me worries. All the good eating seemed to be lodging in little bulges of flesh on my hips and upper thighs, quite the wrong emphasis for a dancer. For years a spare slim creature, I could not really believe that my shape was altering in this way. But the evidence was there, daily, in mirrors at class and in hotel bedrooms. I was not pleased. And for the next eighteen months the graph of my zig-zag morale followed more or less the inflating and deflating of my shape, a correlative not causal relationship. Both were strongly affected by the wavering fortunes of *la vie de danse.*

I came home to Edinburgh via London with a sense of considerable triumph. Although I had not achieved nearly as much as I had hoped in actual dancing, I felt I had done all right in looking after myself in a reasonably adult fashion during this first experience of prolonged travel. I had managed my money, I had not missed trains or got lost. I had not left my possessions scattered across Europe, I had made sensible arrangement about leaving my trunk in Paris and supplying the hotel with forwarding addresses. Apart from the one débacle at Cairo, I had not left my parents anxious as to my whereabouts. In short, I had kept my head above water in new and often perplexing circumstances.

I had also made one or two warm friends in the company, notably Geneviève, charming generous Geneviève who came from a wealthy family and had a small square humorous face like Katherine Hepburn, a magnificent bust, a funny diminutive torso and legs, and a splendid sense of fun. The only thing I could neither stand nor understand about Geneviève was her choice of lover, a tall elderly Frenchman, well-heeled and to my eyes totally unattractive, another instance of the little friend-ageing protector relationship I found so amazing. How could such a superbly attractive young woman give herself to this old turkey-faced creature? Henri and I did not strike a particularly cordial relationship with each other when he came for a week to Cannes. Since my personal reactions are, and always have been, embarrassingly easily read in my face, over which I never seem to have acquired the usual masking facilities that other people have, he probably picked up my low opinion of him. And I in my turn did not find him endearing when he said that for him no woman was desirable who did not have a large full bust. Kind Geneviève quickly contradicted him—'Not at all, Henri—Many other things count—hips, beautiful legs—'. This was tactful, for legs were my strong point, bust unimpressive for those philistine sweater-girl days.

I spent a few days in the luxurious Avenue Victor Hugo apartment belonging to Geneviève's parents on my way home through Paris, and then made for London where once again I was the guest of my father's old Dublin friends. It was here that I realised how much I had gained in personal confidence, for when the usual inquisition about the kind of wines we were drinking started, I scored almost as well as if I'd known the right answers. With forthright indifference I replied: 'I have no idea' and looked Uncle Frank straight in the eyes as I said it.

Back in Edinburgh my parents, of course, gave me a huge welcome. But for the first hour or two, sitting in the bay window of that changeless sitting room, I was struck with an acute attack of traveller's reticence, a strong antipathy to the idea of sharing with them my experiences. Perhaps I felt, quite correctly, that much would have to be subtly distorted, translated into the idiom we all shared at home. I had had, more distinctively than ever before, my own experiences which were not their experiences, and were moreover quite outside anything they had known. However, there was an obligation to 'tell' and share. And in the all-important need for family solidarity, I would (and did) offer a gloss on these experiences as if I had gone through them as nothing but a family member. I would fit them into the shorthand of descriptive phrases we used among ourselves, making them over into the kind of private humour which alone was safe for us to suggest to each other as the way we saw the world. Traumatic moments would be turned into comedy, angst and melancholy would be omitted entirely, partly through pride, partly to perpetuate this image of super-resilience which my mother needed, and which, I think, I felt was a condition of her totally uncritical affection for me.

Somehow I found my confidence ebbing during that visit home, my first conscious (or semi-conscious) experience of the dangerously draining effect of feeding one's personal reality into the structure of someone else's fantasy. Nothing live comes out in return, only the too-seductive assurance of one's continuing specialness, also fantasy, and miserably unsupportive. Yet I was foolish enough to go on for many years playing this game of offering myself to remote starved people (of both sexes) who had no intention or capacity to taste reality for themselves. And by 'reality' in this context I mean the mismatch between private illusion and actual experience. That I was myself partly unwilling to face that discomfort is clear from continuing to play the role of 'feeder'.

During the weeks in Edinburgh I was starting to realise that my immersion in a life so very different was bound to move me away from people I loved very much. (Also, I suspect, there was the reminder that life at home was infinitely easier, safer, and less overtly complex, and perhaps it was not until I had time to pause that the stressfulness of the last few months came home to roost.) The idea of acknowledging this inevitable separation I found very threatening. I wanted my family to remain the people who knew best, whose understanding was to be relied upon. Yet I knew, at some level, that it was wishful thinking to go on believing the world was as simple as they would have it, that there were far too many circumstances when the projection of the Russell world view was a vastly misleading map to follow. I did not manage to square up to this lurking insight, and the result was a growing tension within myself.

There was another factor. In my family there was very little means of coping with doubt. Doubt was so strongly present and so threatening that to allay the fears of this area of chaos and anarchy we all expressed ourselves with tremendous certainty and clarity, to the point of dogmatism. It was more marked on the female side. My father, most of whose life had kept within situations which, however dramatic in themselves, like famine and sporadic rioting, could be handled within a known frame of reference, admitted that he was not given to questioning his beliefs or their origins. But my mother lived in a sea of such troubling uncertainties that a barrier of cast-iron quality in the way of morals, simplistic ethics and ways of seeing had to be forever reinforced against this menace. There was no freedom to question, above all to raise the vital possibility that such a search for certainty was a falsifying and ultimately forlorn quest.

I see many families, not only my own, as sad little seige structures of the personal, trying hard to hold out against the threats of a world governed by different, or worst of all, no principles. They exist for themselves, and little else, small loving cannibalistic allegiances, in which the unforgivable sin is for an individual member to turn even partial stranger. Such families—and they have their enormous seductions—operate with exquisite and unsuspecting finesse a double-bind round the issue of individualism. Of course its members must be individuals with 'character' and assertiveness and a zest for achievement. This ensures the vitality of the group. But any serious process of self-discovery, in the sense that Jung speaks of 'individuation', be it through intellectual questioning or an attempt to develop creative powers, is sanctioned out of existence with a well-chosen repertoire of pragmatic derision and a degree of consciousness which operates like a Gorgon's head. The ethos is powerfully and successfully uncongenial to a certain kind of seriousness—mainly of commitment to anything but the fostering and strengthening of this particular family. It is heresy to place anything—art, politics, scientific research, sexuality (that above all) as the prior passion to the family.

For these families are in fact places of passion; dark, gloomy, defensive passion, the place where the passionate but fearful hope to have found a safe expression for their feelings, where this potent force will not blow their world up in their faces. Instead it blows its members up like giant inflatables, hoping by this compensation to slide past the knowledge that the family stage is tiny and ludicrous, and the scope of action self-limited. So the confusing message to the offspring is: 'Go out and achieve and succeed, my dear, we expect it of you. But mind you don't acquire any skill, or technique, or knowledge, or have any inspirational experiences which put you outside our reach. Do not, above all, let yourself be changed by your experiences.'

The long arm of family feeling. For some reason it gripped me more tightly on my second trip abroad than on my first. When I went back to Paris my mother came over with me for a couple of weeks' holiday. It was not a very harmonious experience, and I was left with the feeling I had not treated her very well, which indeed I had not. The simple truth was that I don't think I wanted her around in 'my' city. Nor was I quite as emancipated and confident as perhaps I had made out in my travellers' tales back home. Paris, much though I loved it, could still be intimidating. There was that need to have a slight fighting edge, and generally to shed polite British restraint in order to hold one's own. I resented having to carry my mother to a certain extent, and resented spending time with her when I wanted to be off with Malcolm, my former love, who had by this time turned up in Paris to try his luck as a casual English-language teacher—with some idea, I suppose, of starting the literary life, for it was at this time that he came out with his pitiful admission that he did not know whether his destiny was to be Shakespeare, Dickens, or the scum of the earth.

I did, in fact, ditch my mother for longer periods than were kind, while Malcolm and I tried to revive the fast-cooling ardours of our earlier relationship. With hindsight, I am aware how pathetically very young couples unnerve each other by expecting too much in the way of assurance and coping behaviour, how much diminished people can be by an unfamiliar setting. Malcolm, being new and nervous and hardly speaking French, could hardly be the bold virile figure that he had been for me in Edinburgh. And I, no doubt, would hardly shine with the same glamour in Paris, where ever second young person one met was doing something unusual in the way of a career, or bumming around more or less picturesquely. My disillusionment with Malcolm reminds me of a story by Francois Mauriac about a teenage couple who elope. It is one of the most depressing stories I've read, and exactly captures that dismal forlorn insecurity of very young lovers whose passion is totally unproof against the mutual resent that neither has the strength to reassure the other.

We had also reached an impasse which nowadays would have been quite differently resolved—though whether this would have hastened or held back the process of disentangling I don't know. Although we lay with our arms round each other on the bed in his unromantic cheap room, layers and layers of Edinburgh-induced restraints and fears protected us—or at least me—far more effectively than the clothes I would not shed. We were both too shy and tentative and distrustful of each other to see past the old associations of school-uniformed daring when holding hands and kissing were the ultimate in passionate expression. There was also a sharp practical consideration. I did not know the first thing about contraception. If Malcolm did, he could not get to the point of voicing it. So we wrestled rather wearily with desire whose strength seemed out of key with the qualified kind of emotions that went with it.

I think I was singularly ungenerous towards him, not because I resisted becoming his lover, but because I failed to behave nicely as an old friend who might have been expected to help him over the first few weeks in a strange place, and instead was impatient and demanding. When his brother Roderick also showed up a little later, the same impatience, the same reluctance to acknowledge our old friendship was there. Perhaps I simply resented Edinburgh catching up with me in Paris. There must, in fact, have been a fairly strong sense of split and incompatability which I was not the only person to experience. I have already mentioned Barbara, my musical friend on a student scholarship and our inability to strike the same note of friendship in Edinburgh. It was something to do with the ease of response in Paris to the place itself, and its statement that cities are, or should be, places of lighthearted beauty as well as toil or the erecting of façades of respectability. To admit to 'loving' Paris was to admit to a generalised erotic sense which had nothing to do with on-the-ground relationships, but spoke of a capacity in oneself which had firmly to be stubbed out in the context of Edinburgh. Coming back from Paris to Edinburgh always poses acute re-entry problems.

I felt alternately conscious-stricken and impatient with my mother, the first signs, no doubt, of adolescent distancing which till then I had shown so little sign of developing. My exasperation with her reached a high crescendo during a visit to the Musée Rodin, my first exposure, as it was hers, to the powerful extroverted passion of his work. I was amazed, startled, bemused, and the last thing I felt competent to do was to give the lucid little thumbnail appraisals which she was mutely but insistently demanding. With infuriating persistence, she trotted after me and stood meekly waiting, a hint of caricature about her obedient pupil act as she breathed rather fast and waited patiently to be instructed. It was phony and ridiculous and worst of all I couldn't play up to it. So I kept striding on faster and faster hoping to shake her off and have a bit of peace to look for myself. And still she followed.

Years later I asked her if she remembered that visit, and whether she realised how irritating I had found her. She remembered it quite distinctly. 'I knew I was making you mad,' she said. 'But I couldn't stop myself.' I still feel baffled, until I remember instances of trapping myself in unrewarding obsessional behaviour, which shed no light on the problem but at least supply a corrective to the attitude that 'she could have had the sense to stop'. I, perhaps should have had the good sense to say: 'For God's sake, stop being such an idiot. I don't know any more than you which of these works is Baedecker one, two or three star.' Maybe all innocently—or even not so innocently —she was challenging that damned role of aesthetic expert which I'd been partly lumbered with, partly appropriated.

But such minor strains and frictions did not alter matters greatly. My letters home thereafter and for all the time I was abroad continued to be full of affection, and it was genuinely meant. Certainly they did not give a very accurate picture of my life, which would have been surprising, but there was no slackening in my strong feelings for both my parents.

148

It was after my mother's return to Edinburgh that the blow fell. Every possible disaster had overtaken the Ballets des Champs Elysées. Having been cut off from all sources of rumour and gossip during my mother's visit, it was not until I went to the theatre to find out when rehearsals for the grand Australian tour were due to start that I had any idea things were amiss. I was waylaid by some of the dancers before I ever got near the administration, and over coffees in the little cafe opposite I heard the dismal sequence of events. There had been a major row between principals and administration which had resulted in Jean Babilée and Irène Skorik leaving—two major attractions for the proposed tours which had had to be cancelled without them. Roger Eudes had withdrawn his financial support leaving the company penniless, and to cap all, Youly Algaroff, the other male star dancer had got ill and was diagnosed as having tuberculosis. In short, there was no more Ballets des Champs Elysées. I and the others sitting round the table were now out of work and I, if no one else, was far from home.

That was some time in May. There followed a long hot weary summer. I had no intention of giving in and going back home. I wrote my parents that I would try for an audition with Roland Petit's Ballets de Paris, and that meanwhile I would continue to go to morning class at the Salles Wacker with Madame Egorova and give English lessons in the afternoon to make some money. I would economise by eating only one main meal a day. I exhorted them not to feel too depressed, or to worry, something that I did repeatedly in letters from then on, as if their wellbeing were my responsibility. In fact, it is a timely reminder, to re-read my letters home. For I have often wondered how it was, as things got more and more precarious, that my very solicitous parents weren't provoked into telling me for goodness sake to get out of a bad situation and come home. But one gets, more or less, what one asks for. In those bulletins which I sent from time to time I put on an act of confidence and resilience, making a wry humorous story of the struggling company's endless changes of plan and the diet of unsubstantiated hopes on which we were fed, doing my best to hide the fits of melancholy and depression behind a facade of bravado and coping.

In the event, I gave no English lessons, and I did not get into the Ballets de Paris. A mob of more than a hundred out-of-work dancers showed up for the audition, and I was not the one chosen. Meanwhile, with the extraordinary tenacity which kept some sort of company going off and on for another two years, the administrator, Jean Robin, whom we all heartily disliked but had to admire for refusal to give in, had scraped together a month's season at the Théatre des Champs Elysées. Yvette Chauviré, *danseuse étoile* at the Paris Opera, was to guest with us, and we were hastily reassembled with some additions, and started rehearsals. But most of my friends of the last tour had left. Tutti was no longer there, Geneviève had disappeared. Nicky Polajaenko and his demanding mistress had also gone.

As far as official history goes, the Ballets des Champs Elysées ceased at that point, in 1950. This is the date given in the various reference books on dance. Yet these said books are not entirely consistent, for under the biographies of individual dancers and choreographers, it appears that they worked for the Ballets des Champs Elysées, or produced ballets in 1951. And I can vouch for the fact that a dance company under that name certainly continued to perform at intervals until early 1952. But without a doubt it was a kind of ghost company. From that major upheaval which had caused the exit of its key members in all directions, it never recovered, however many distinguished performers graced it in the passing. The core of the company was gone, its spirit broken.

By this time I had moved my living quarters from the old Hotel Avenida to a quiet little street in Passy, and had become part of the ménage of magnificent Madame Schopfer, widow of a Swiss, and herself half American, half French. Her flat was a kind of lodging *en famille* for girls coming from abroad to study in Paris, especially those with musical inclinations. It was through my friend Barbara, the singing student, that I heard of her, and had my first and only taste of ordinary middle-class French domestic living arrangements, with a concierge sitting tortoise-like in the little peep-hole room of the ground floor flat, and a lift which one could use for going up but not for coming down, and which all too frequently had the dispiriting black-lettered notice '*L'ascenseur ne marche pas*' hung from its grilled gate. Inside Madame Schopfer's apartment there was an air of modestly genteel gloom, but its windows gave a most magnificent view over Paris and the Seine, and often I watched in a mild trance while the sunset faded and the colouring changed every five minutes and the lights came on with a soft twinkle which roused obscure feelings of muzzy poetry.

We gathered at mealtimes, three or four of us girls, round an oblong table flanked by the erect, firm Edwardian figure of Madame Schopfer at one end and at the other by small sagging gentle Madame Fol, widows who had lived together for many years. Their relationship by this time was not harmonious, soured by events within the family. Madame Schopfer's only daughter had married Madame Fol's son, and it was some time after this event that the two ladies had decided to share a dwelling. All had gone well until the marriage broke up, the errant partner being Madame Fol's son who had left his wife in the embittering position of single parent with two sons to raise. Certainly by the time we knew them the relationship between the two elderly ladies had set into a permanent and not very pleasant kind of dominance-submission. Madame Fol, bent, humble and slow-spoken, was treated by Madame Schopfer as a sort of buffoon. Her efforts to be helpful were dismissed as fumbling and ridiculous, her opinions, when ventured, sniffed at scornfully. The story of the broken marriage, when I was told it by one of the girls, substantitated the sense of permanent punitiveness which coloured the attitude of Madame Schopfer.

She was in any case a very different sort of old lady, and in spite of her rather cruel victimisation of poor little Madame Fol (who, I suspect, came from nearer the peasant end of the social scale) one couldn't help liking and admiring her. She had a small wryly pursed mouth, suggesting down-to-earn humour, and a neat little snub nose, none of which detracted from the dignity of her elaborately coiffed white hair and her poker straight back, which recalled old photos of Queen Mary. Indeed, there was something queenly about her, and her strong, outgoing personality conveyed the idea that she knew well how to hold her own in sophisticated society. Her connection with the musical world was strong, and her daughter, inappropriately nicknamed 'Biche', which means 'deer', was accompanist for some of Paris's leading singers of the time, in particular the handsome baritone, Gerard Souzay. Biche was a tall, homely woman with a curious set of rake-like teeth, and as little evocative of the quiet grace associated with her nickname as it was possible to be. However, it was at her apartment that I met the impressive Gerard Souzay in person at a reception after a concert at the Salle Gaveau, and also on the same occasion fled in confused terror from her son, an up-and-coming jazz musician, a curiously attractive though pallid and fleshy young man who was scorching me with looks so blatantly lustful that, once again, I was unnerved to the point of retreat. Later, I regretted this. Unlike previous retreats, this one was also a flight from my own sexual feelings, which I knew as little how to deal with as I knew about dealing with others' desires. Hubert's enormous suggestive eyes put me in a panic—maybe I was afraid that if I responded at all I would fling myself into his arms then and there.

Madame Schopfer saw it as part of her duty to improve our knowledge of French round her dinner table, a directive which produced the usual squirming embarrassment that nationals feel when expected to perform to each other in a foreign tongue. I feel sure that she introduced all sorts of improving subjects, but the only one that sticks vividly in my memory is to do with her own health. The French have particularly picturesque ways of being in ill-health. On this occasion we were astounded by an account of the crumbling of the vertebrae in Madame Schopfer's neck. These were, it seemed, in the process of decalcification and were reforming themselves into a pathological structure which she described as a *'bec de perroquet'*—parrot's beak. The very idea of anything being at fault with that magnificently upright stem was difficult to accept, and that it should be concealing anything so aberrant as a parrot's beak was even more incredible. Yet with precision and dignity Madame simultaneously gave us a lecture on bone deterioration and French pronunciation—I still have the sound of her carefully separated syllables in my ears, 'la dé-cal-ci-fi-ca-tion du cou', being careful to point out to us the contrast between the vowel sounds in 'du' and 'cou'. All this over paté maison and ragout washed down with diluted red wine.

It was also at Madame Schopfer's that I met Odette and Peter Churchill, then still man and wife. Madame Schopfer, if not actively engaged in the Resistance (and for all I know she may have been), had certainly provided a friendly port of call. She and the Churchills had not met since the war until this occasion, when Barbara and I, rather honoured by being present, listened in silence to the three of them catching up on their wartime experiences. Peter Churchill said little, letting the amazingly forceful Odette tell her tale of risk-fraught missions which eventually ended with her capture. How, Madame Shopfer wanted to know, had she managed to survive in prison? Hadn't she been tortured? Odette passed fairly quickly over the last question, admitting with that extraordinary French matter-of-factness which suggests the subject is hardly worth bothering about, that she had had fingernails and toenails pulled out and one or two other matters which made us shiver. But as to the solitary confinement, her astonishing reply was that sometimes she felt that the days had not been long enough for her to think about all that was in her mind. She set herself elaborate fantasy tasks, like making entire wardrobes of clothes, stitch by stitch, for her three little girls, refurnishing their home, replanning the garden, an amazing recital of inner resource and discipline. It had helped, she said, that she had already had the experience as a child of being blind for a prolonged period.

They came round for a second visit, and this time Madame Schopfer had also invited the woman who ran the embroidery shop just along the street. She had been in the same prison as

Odette. After the first amazement of reunion they started up an intense argument about their present attitudes towards the Germans. The little embroidery woman remained blazing with hate against *les Boches*. 'If I had a German baby in my arms,' she said passionately, 'I would dash its head against the curb'. 'No, no,' protested Odette, 'I would want to bring it up with totally non-German ideas.' She went on to expound her philosophy of gentle liberal education, but she was not, in essence, a gentle person. How could she be, with the force to do what she had done? Barbara and I crept away from these encounters and shared our sense of shame that this appalling war had passed over our lives hardly causing a tremor. Our unawareness seemed, in the face of the kinds of experiences we had been listening to, a kind of petty nose-thumbing at the forces of history. Lucky we had been, but ignorant we would remain (and therefore lacking a dimension perhaps essential to understand our present world) of what it is like to have all sense of personal destiny swept into irrelevance by the violent tide of total war.

For all her contact with the world of art and music (Jacqueline Matisse, granddaughter of the painter, was another intermittent lodger) Madame Schopfer was not the easiest of landladies to team up with the infinite unpredictability of ballet-company life. Why I continued as long as I did the ridiculous arrangement of doubling back to Passy for a mid-day meal, I don't know, except that it was probably part of the terms of my *pension* arrangement. Inevitably I was hours late because morning class followed by rehearsal had overrun its alloted time. Every time I had to face her amazed indignation, directed ostensibly at the company but rubbing off on me, of course. Trivial though it sounds, this strain started to wear on me, and one day I had a fit of weeping at rehearsal so violent that even cold Marika, still our ballet-mistress, decided she had better find out what was the trouble. There was no very precise trouble. I was reacting, I suppose, to a whole bunch of things, mainly to do with the permanent uncertainty of the present existence, along with the physical strain of dancing in the heat of an unusually hot summer. Paris in summer becomes exceedingly thundery. In August, everyone, sensibly, removes themselves. But even earlier the build-up of tension can be intense. Many a time my watchings from Madame Shopfer's window were of spectacular storms with forked lightning running helter-skelter across the skyline between the *grandes éclairages* of sheet lightning. It was awe-inspiring. Barbara, not normally a nervous person, begged me not to wash my hair during a particularly violent storm, as I intended, in case I got electrocuted.

It was certainly not a happy summer. Consciously, I could not face what I am quite sure my intuitions were telling me, that I was adrift. The blow to the ballet company had affected me severely. Gone the opportunities for travel across the world, the mild glamour of the previous tour, the sense of belonging to a company with a name to conjure with. There was no borrowed prestige to be got from a reduced demoralised group struggling for survival. Nor had I been with it long enough to draw on a sense of loyalty and history which some at least of the remaining members felt. There was not a soul in the ballet world in Paris who took any kind of personal interest in my work or my progress. I had not attended any teacher for more than a few weeks, far too short a time to establish that kind of link, and I was not an exceptional enough dancer to shine out, except occasionally, from the dozens of good experienced professionals who thronged the studios.

In any case, the whole ballet scene then (whatever it is now) was full of bubble ventures which lasted all of a few weeks, sometimes not as long, a new impresario showing above the horizon for a brief spell before succumbing to the financial impossibilities of ventures sketched out with such grandiose confidence. I auditioned, and was accepted, for two or three tours with new groups which never got further off the ground than an occasional gala in Paris, pitifully paid, a few television performances, although talk of Spain, Scandinavia, Germany, etc. had filled our ears and our hopes.

155

For the next eighteen months, broken with occasional returns home to Edinburgh to recuperate, I lived in a state of constant uncertainty, with a series of projected ventures, dangled maddeningly like some ephemeral carrot, always about to happen. The semi-ghostly Ballets des Champs Elysées was one of the main tantalisers. Rather than let their core of dancers disperse entirely, we were kept forever on tenterhooks with a fascinating if unsubstantial sequence of intrigues, negotiations, half-promises from backers, tours about to happen, 'in the pipeline', and so on. And just as one was starting to lose faith, lo and behold! they would actually produce a proper plan, a contract for a tour, for all of a few weeks, and off we would go again. I am quite sure it has conditioned me for the rest of my life to the notion that it is impossible ever to look well ahead into the future.

Meanwhile, equally impossible to face squarely, the sense of my temperamental 'all-wrongness' for a life in ballet was pressed upon me from various friendly sources, one of the most persuasive being a curious little officer in the French army, a passionate Scottophile whom I had met at the Caledonian Club which I still went to from time to time. Bernard, a scion of a titled family, was a lovable if rather ridiculous little grasshopper of a man, who took a tender interest in my welfare. Because he was lively and amusing, I did not immediately realise how intensely conventional his ideas were. He clearly felt that ballet, for *une jeune fille bien,* was a near neighbour of prostitution, and was much concerned that I should be moving among this bohemian horde. But he took my commitment seriously enough to make what was for him a mighty step into polluted territory. He actually arranged to meet Yvette Chauviré, who had starred with us for our brief cobbled-together Paris summer season. And Bernard left me in no doubt as to the distastefulness of his task—he, a correct officer of the French army, having to ask the favour of an interview with a ballet dancer (though I would have thought that her fame and charm might have sugared the pill slightly). Her verdict was: 'She has talent, but needs a great deal more basic training.' The first half of the statement may or may not have been true, but about the accuracy of the second there was no doubt. Where I was exceedingly out of luck, both in the kind of company I had joined, and in its sad downward swing, was that there was no idea of training up its younger dancers. In its best days there was a kind of anarchic vigour. In its dusty days survival was the first concern, and that meant sweating the last out of the fewest possible number.

If I was to progress beyond my present state, I needed to be taken in hand, removed from the scene of touring which is desperately taxing and can erode the standards of the best, and simply go back to the classroom. Which meant money. There wasn't any. My parents weren't willing—and I don't blame them—to face another dose of major expense for training. Yet the whole business of a dancer keeping in training puts her or him in a different and more difficult position than other artists. Singers and musicians doubtless need their tuition. They can, however, to some extent keep in practice on their own. A dancer cannot. The daily class is essential. Home practice is impossible. Even if the self-discipline is there the space is not.

So, in a state of very dubious morale and physically tired out, I left with the company for a month's tour of Israel, in mid-July of an exceptionally hot summer. It was, by and large, infernal. The last thing I could now complain of was being underworked, though none of the promised solo work came my way, and I was feeling too depressed and low to take up the matter. We were based in Tel Aviv, and gave most of our performances in the amphitheatre at Caesarea outside the town, often giving matinees as well as evening performances. But we also went to Haifa and Jerusalem, both of which towns I found infinitely preferable to raw, new Tel Aviv, where the evidence of a town in the making was abundant. I had never stepped outside a 'finished' city. Roundabouts and traffic junctions marked off by oil drums, buildings being run up like card-houses with much the same outlines, a hotel where basic amenities like water and air-conditioning were subject to freakish interruption, were all new and unpleasant phenomena. After performances away from Tel

Aviv we faced a three to four hour journey back to base in a bus which seemed to have been made without springs—or perhaps it was the effect of the stony rutted roads—arriving in the early hours of the morning to fling ourselves exhausted into bed. We drank endless soft drinks, and poured them all out in rivers of sweat. Make-up felt like wearing a sticky non-porous sock over one's face, and my skin quickly broke into a protesting rash of spots which did nothing to raise my spirits. The curiosity about my surroundings which had flavoured that first now poignantly distant tour was totally gone. I think the only cultural detail which registered with some sense of lively surprise was breakfast. I had never met salad of cucumbers, peppers, tomatoes and cream cheese at this hour of the day. And the one gourmet experience was the magnificent yoghourt which we ate copiously and continuously.

I have faint memories of pleasant experiences, the occasional party or reception, a company dinner in an open-air restaurant on Mount Carmel overlooking the port of Haifa twinkling seductively in its lamplight, being taken out to a night-club by a young Israeli from the British Consulate, buying some pretty pieces of turquoise-studded silver jewellery. But on the whole that tour is marked by a sense of nightmarish discomfort and strain, coupled with a strong sense of British unpopularity and vivid local memories of our occupation of Palestine.

Towards the end, my run-down state manifested itself in the burgeoning of an enormous abscess on my thigh, against which tights chafed agonisingly. More in pieces than together I got back to Paris, briefly collected together my luggage, and headed for home, abandoning various pleasant options like holidaying with French friends, or going to Cannes to stay with one of my fellow-dancers who had invited me to her home. Bedraggled, ill, and looking a spotted wreck of my former self, I arrived in Edinburgh, where a first priority was to get that abscess, now stretching its swelling from hip to knee, attended to.

The family doctor at that time was a surly, red-faced, old-schooler, who did not believe in patients taking too articulate an interest in their complaints. I was put on massive doses of penicillin, prescribed in gruff silence. 'Will this prevent me going on dancing?' I asked, and it was a curious question to ask, because abscesses are not like injuries and could be assumed, even one of this size, to heal up. I'm fairly certain the question had a double and contradictory motivation. All passionate to be reassured that dancing was not in danger at one level, some small creature inside, feeling it had had more than it bargained for, was asking to be let off the hook—honourably. With the practised GP's skill in evading point-blank questions, I got no satisfaction either way.

Three weeks or so later, a picture of me appeared in the *Evening News* (tipped off, no doubt, by the journalist friend whose blue eyes had been worthy of record in my fifteen-year-old journal) sitting demurely in my parents' home, tartan skirt well displayed, with a tutu on my lap and a sea of point-shoes over the carpet. The caption runs something to the effect that 'Edinburgh-trained Una Russell asked for a job with a French ballet company, and got it. She is seen here making a few repairs to her fragile ballet dress while she rests between tours.' To be accurate, I was at that point a good deal more fragile than the ballet dress, but this piece of publicity served to perpetuate the ridiculous myth of the brave, buccaneering lass who was making good, and by the autumn I was back in Paris again.

Hard Times

Not one firm clue remains in my memory as to how this decision to return to France was reached, whether I obeyed some migratory instinct to make again for Paris, a city which still drew me powerfully despite the disconsolate summer I had spent there, or whether, as is quite possible, I received a letter from the company asking me to rejoin for a tour of France scheduled for November. I do not know if the decision was reached in family conclave, or in consultation with Marjorie Middleton to whose studio I had returned to get into practice again once my abscess had healed. What rationale was applied that came out in favour of returning I have no idea.

By the time I returned the company had acquired a new impresario, a slender young man with a small prissy mouth and dark glasses who took an instant and cordial detestation to me. While this did not interfere much with everyday life it was, to say the least, unfortunate. Enemies among those who are in a position to give jobs are best avoided. As guest stars for this tour there were Vladimir Skouratoff, a devilishly handsome Russian *étoile,* and his current mistress, Jacqueline Moreau, ex-première danseuse of the Paris Opera ballet. Moreau was a hard, technically showy dancer with about as much dramatic talent as a Christmas tree fairy. Far more popular among the company members was the other ballerina, Sonia Arova, a far better artist, but to meet still credibly a Bulgarian peasant with good-humoured blunt snub features and curious wide-set eyes. She brought mama on tour, which added to the peasant touch, for mama was vast, black-clad, spoke little French and simply smiled a huge smile like a benevolent toad. My friend and room-mate on this tour was Hélène Trailine, another white Russian, who was a première danseuse. Helen's dancing was correct and basically uninspired. The gap between her poor performances and her good ones was never dramatically large. But she was a pleasant companion, and took me under her wing very kindly.

I will not enter into another prolonged recital of touring woes. This tour was a winter version of the Israeli experience. We covered something like twenty-eight towns all over France in one month, which meant that more often than not we were travelling overnight in the touring coach. I started to detest this enforced group life and became more and more morose and inturned. Tours, I discovered, had an either-or effect. Either one became more gregarious, in a high edgy sort of way, hepped up by the constant movement and short time spans, or the reverse happened. On this one I got to the point where it was immaterial which town we were in, for all we ever saw was backstage in the theatre, a hotel bedroom if we were lucky enough to be staying overnight, and a restaurant. Night-time travel was sometimes interrupted if we happened to pass an inn still with its lights on, at which point we would all tumble out into the dark, troop in for a drink and snack and a quick pee in slightly more comfortable conditions than squatting beside the roadside. Though even that was uncertain—at one such stop the latrines (no other word will do) were several hundred yards away from the inn at the bottom of a muddy field. After stumbling round in the dark, one came eventually to two evil smelling sheds with the classic meagreness of equipment of archaic French plumbing—two 'footprints' of concrete straddling a hole in the ground, surely one of the most fundamental expressions of male chauvinism ever to be incorporated into functional design. By the time we (mostly the women) had lost and found our way there and back, our journey was well behind schedule. Finally, the tour ended with us being tipped out at five-thirty in the morning in Paris in mid-December.

Followed ten days of pre-Christmas fun. Jacqueline Matisse kindly put me up in her huge luxurious room, saving me the trouble and expense of booking into an hotel, as I was due shortly to set off for Monte Carlo where Marika, whose protector lived there, had gathered a group of six dancers to perform the ballets during the Christmas season of ballet and opera at the Casino Opera House. Since the ballet company had nothing immediate to offer this seemed a good way of earning some cash. I renewed contact with my friends in Paris, Scottish and French, went to a few nightclubs and just had time to think how good it would be to have a few more opportunities for normal social nightlife, and was off.

And of all the places to avoid in December and January, I thoroughly recommend Monte Carlo. It rained copiously and almost continuously. It was also exceedingly cold, living in houses designed for a predominantly hot sunny climate. Chilly tiled floors, flimsy windows and inadequate little heating stoves turned these fancy villas into draughty purgatories. Palm trees swaying in the bitter wind coming off the sea were also a depressing sight, while the town, layered in its terraces up a hillside, was dead and hibernating save for a few cake shops where we overate through greed and boredom. I looked in vain for any sign of the gay and reckless life reputedly led here. At this time of the year there was not even an echo of it.

The work was, of course, of trifling interest, though we were exercised and worked hard enough. Once again, my slightly uncertain health raised a passing query. Even for such a short contract, we had to undergo the official medical examination insisted on for all employees of the Casino. Having listened to my heart beat, the doctor looked dubious and insisted that I come back for a second checkup before passing me fit. At the second checkup he made me do a quick bout of strenuous exercises, after which he said, still not very enthusiastically, that in spite of the abnormal increase in pulse rate it also returned quite quickly to normal and that probably I was fit enough, but that he would much prefer to see me in a 'more sedentary occupation'. Once more it seemed as though my body was trying to get through a message of protest, which it is curious that I chose to ignore, for I was by no means averse to a bit of self-pity.

Opera ballets are flimsy little things, and Marika's choreography would hardly have scored points for originality, but the dancing was quite enjoyable and there was a certain kudos in being Parisians gracing what was undoubtedly a somewhat parochial outfit. Nevertheless, there were dispiriting factors. I felt I had seen the true rock-bottom of hack performers when I had encountered the local opera chorus of whom I wrote a scathing account to my brother '. . . a most depressing sight, infinitely worse than a *corps de ballet,* where the average age is at least twenty years less, and the average weight at least three or four stone less—I talk of the female side. For as much as the women are hefty, the men are small and wizened. Such a dowdy, shabby, and even dirty lot I have rarely seen, and nothing changes them—make-up, wigs, costumes have no effect on their faces or figures. Beside them the gallant little group of dancers look small and half-starved.'

That may be, but by the time I got back to Paris in February I had put on such an alarming amount of weight that instant action had to be taken. I had gone to Monte Carlo pruned down to skinny nothing after that exhausting tour, and had come back horribly inflated by all those damned cakes we had eaten to alleviate our boredom. Monsieur Robin, our administrator, hinted unkindly that I might be put out of the company unless I lost weight quickly. But kind Youly Algaroff, by this time well enough to act as ballet master, calmed me down and simply suggested I get busy and go on a diet. More soothing words came from Alex, the witty half-English girl who had before this befriended me with hospitality and seen to it that I got some proper grounding in the French classics by lending me her books. 'Don't panic,' she said. 'I'll introduce you to Max, my masseur. He specialises in dancers' weight problems.'

So I was led, wondering but obedient, to a scruffy studio somewhere beyond the Place Pigalle where a mournful muscular man with a balding head and great big powerful hands agreed to give me a course of a dozen massages for some appallingly high sum. Bang went part of my precious Monte Carlo earnings.

Those ill-considered pastries were costing me double, one price to eat and another to have their effects removed.

Max's place was the weirdest combination of work and home. In spite of the high prices he charged there was an air of anything but affluence. The atmosphere was part sports hall, part studio, part massage parlour. It had a gallery running round on all four sides, and on one side there were various curtained partitions which constituted the family home. If my massage appointment was a late one the smells of cooking—tomatoes, peppers, oil, garlic, meat—came wafting down as I lay being pummelled while his wife made supper and scolded their small child. The idea of trying to live a domestic life overlooking the cold gloomy space below was a depressing one, and so was my first experience of the massage treatment. I knew it seemed too easy, just to lie there and be gently manipulated and have the weight fall off, and I was right. The massage was a special sort, very, very painful, more like sustained pinching by very strong hands. The idea was to break up the 'cellulite'—watery fatty globules under the skin, by this kneading and pinching, and so to get rid of it.

I still have no idea whether this is sound practice, and am not in a position to judge the efficacy of Max's method, taken on its own, for I certainly lost weight and lost it fast, but whether it was due to his labours or to the fact that I went on a stringent diet, I don't know. Certainly one of the surest ways of slimming fast is to undergo a painful expensive course of treatment, for the idea of all that money and suffering being wasted is unbearable, and it adds empires of firmness to one's dietary resolves. Twice a week for the next six weeks I lay and clenched my teeth in acute pain while Max's enormous hands pulled at my thighs and slowly ground down the excess flesh. But the results were excellent. My basic good shape started to emerge in newfound clean lines. I bought a specially clinging pair of black practice tights and a new leotard in celebration, and was told by my male colleagues in the company 'Tu redeviens belle!' Thus encouraged I started to take a new pride in my work, also noted, which brought me some solo work when we set off on tour again. For by this time, contrary as ever, the company had managed to pull another rabbit out of the hat, and we were due to go to Germany on a well-paid tour (as much as these things ever were well paid) to decent-sized towns with decent theatres—Munich, Nuremberg, Cassel, Frankfurt, Stuttgart, Berlin and Cologne, among others.

The lead up to this happy turn of events, however, had been slow and uncertain and attended by what was now the routine pattern of hope and doubt. After returning from Monte Carlo the air was full of the usual near-promises of work for the company. There were only the final details to be fixed with a new pair of impresarios, before we would be heading for South America. The news bulletins, passed along the line of dancers preparing for class, changed daily. South America was off, one of the backers was a *salaud* and had tried to make too sharp a deal before pulling out entirely. On the other hand, there was a strong possibility that . . . and so it went on. Furthermore, the glad news that we were at last to receive back pay from the previous summer turned out to be as ephemeral as all the other financial fairy tales with which we were fed. There is something ironic in the combination of French legal fuss which had us all signing handfuls of official papers before we could be given our just dues, and the shrugging detachment with which we were told there was, after all, no money to pay them.

What with the hole blown in my budget by the massage treatment, I was reduced, as I was from time to time, to writing home and asking for a small injection of funds. I hated doing it. The sum I asked this time was, I think, £15 and it was, as always, immediately forthcoming. My mother also helped out loyally all the time I was abroad by sending parcels with much needed pieces of underwear, occasional hand-knitted jumpers, chocolate, even fruit cake, as well as looking after my supply of point shoes.

Since at this point (February and March) the uncertainties of the Champs Elysées plans were showing no signs of resolving themselves I made a determined effort to find other work. Two ventures presented themselves. The first was a new small group financed by a Spanish impresario, for which I auditioned successfully, and immediately got busy rehearsing for the opening gala to be given in honour of a gathering in Paris of the Ministers of the French Colonies, to be followed by a tour in Spain—the land that always turned out to be never-never. Under our young ballet mistress, Françoise Adret, a vigorous practical lady, we had daily class and for the first time for a long while I picked up some contagious enthusiasm. It helped that she thought highly of my work and my style.

The story, brief, ends with the usual fiasco, the crumbling of plans in a welter of confusion about disappearing backers. Our relationship with impresario Montemar began and ended with that damned gala, where I managed nothing more spectacular than to knock myself senseless at the ball which followed it. During some hectic group samba I skidded on the marble floor, fell backwards, and passed out clean and cold. A nurse was eventually summoned, but by this time I was already starting to come round and she lost interest when she realised that there was no blood flowing and left me to resume dancing with a lump of classic egg-like proportions on the back of my head.

With disgust I described in a letter home the treatment we had received—or failed to receive—from our impresario. '. . . Not only did that brute leave us standing without a table or food or drink, while he went and drank champagne with his friends, but he didn't even get us taxis to go home in, as he'd promised. We were right out of Paris, miles beyond the Bastille and no way of getting home, so we had to wait until the metro started up again.' I got home ultimately at 7 a.m., with a splitting headache and the added complication of a mild state of concussion after that fall. Next day I couldn't remember where I was and kept trying to get Edinburgh telephone numbers through the hotel telephonist, a shaky little old lady who was agitatedly convinced that I had gone mad.

Having my suspicions about the durability of the Montemar outfit, I had also auditioned and been accepted for a company being formed to go to Barcelona starring Tamara Toumanova, with a mixed repertoire of classical and modern ballets. I felt justifiably pleased over this, for all the dancers at the audition seemed to be on hob-knobbing terms with the auditioning panel except myself. When this, too, collapsed I was hit with an appalling depression, which nearly had me throwing my hand in and going home in disgust. But at that moment the fortunes of the Champs Elysées bettered at least to the extent of the German tour, and I rejoined them.

It was during this barren stretch, February to April, when winter had sapped vitality to its lower limits and strikes were stopping metros and buses for days on end and all of us dancers were scraping our pockets that I discovered the communal ménage in downtown St Paul, where penury had its lighter side. Two of the dancers in the company lived there, Gayle, a rake-thin talented American dancer with a sharp undancerish intelligence, and Jacques, one of the old faithfuls of the male corps-de-ballet. The flat they inhabited was owned, and lived in, by a strange man called Maurice, who had for a while been secretary to the Champs Elysées company but had long since gone his own way, which was, as far as I could see, to sit and read and dream and be endlessly kind to dancers down on their luck. What he did for money I have no idea. From time to time he had a little more than the rest of us. But the apartment, whose population grew and shrank as wanderers touched down and moved off again, carried every sign of poverty—bare, shabby, and dirty with a dangerously improvised electrical wiring system. The only thing it had in some abundance was books—it was there that I read one quiet afternoon a French translation of Oscar Wilde's *De Profundis*, an all too appropriate choice for this depressing time.

The flat, however, was not a sombre place, it was a refuge, and the only area of personal privacy I had access to—a bleak little hotel bedroom I do not count. It was a place where one could let one's hair down, in an atmosphere of crazy affectionate fun, where poverty was treated as a joke and a much better one if the little we had was shared around. There were periodic 'cooking nights', when several of us would go round each bringing something towards the meal—cheese, wine, candles, fruit, while

Maurice produced his staple dish of casseroled tuna fish, a delicious savoury concoction to which we gave a suitably pompous menu title—*thon à l'étouffé.* It was part of the joke of high living which was mimicked with tongue-in-cheek solemnity, the table set ceremoniously with many candles in saucers and bottles plumb in the middle of the bare room with its splotched and mouldy walls. One evening it had as centrepiece a tiny fountain with a jet of water playing all of six inches above the table's surface, the result of hours of labour by Maurice and Jacqueau which had wreathed the room in length upon length of fine piping, so that walking across it was like picking one's way through a giant unravelled skein of wool. It must have been all the toasts we drank to the ingenuity of its inventors which put the skids under that particular evening, for it slithered happily into a haze of wine, candle-grease, tuna-fish stew and heat. Some time in the small hours, long after the talk had stopped and we had lain around in various pairs on divans while the candles guttered, I found myself in a bed, too tired and drunk and thankful to wonder how I'd got there, but still able to notice that the sheets were a quiet flannel-grey with dirt. Still later, someone climbed in beside me, whom I just managed to register was Maurice. Slightly inconvenienced, I moved over to one side and resumed my exhausted wine-soaked sleep. Poor Maurice, I was vaguely aware, spent a restless night. Every now and then he moved towards me and tried to put his arms round me, only to receive a sharp repulse and a request to be left alone. Gentlemanly as ever, he retired to the other side of the bed. But a little later, and repeatedly, the same thing would happen again with the same response. In the morning he very courteously begged my pardon for having disturbed me.

Such heartless naïvety makes me wonder whether I was not mentally retarded with regard to sex. But as well as a general reluctance to face the facts of desire,with Maurice there was the additional rigid exclusion which youth operates towards older people. He was not so very old, in his mid or late thirties, perhaps. But as much as I had attended to the matter at all, I imagine I had categorised him as 'past it', at least where young girls were concerned, and considered our relationship to be avuncular in nature. If I could find him now I would want to tell him that he was one of the most gentle and thoughtful people I ever met, and that I'm sorry he got such shabby treatment from me. He deserved better on another occasion, too, several months later when armed with a little money he asked me if I would like to have a proper meal out, to cheer me up? I said yes, eagerly, and ate my way through his generosity, using him throughout the evening to pour out my emotions about a young Englishman with whom I was in love. Maurice, lean, brown and creased, with a wide thin mouth and a funny ugly charming face, listened patiently, playing the older confidante with grave attention, and never once tried to draw the situation round to himself. I would like to say sorry for that too. Being young may be a vulnerable state in many ways, but I hate remembering the cutting edge it gave over older people in the sex game, and how I didn't bother to soften it.

Pause for Reflection

I am still left wondering why I stayed on. Why on earth did I remain in a situation which was so bleak in every direction? Professionally it was clear that Paris was overstocked with good dancers on the job hunt. Socially, I was in the limbo which descends on people who are itinerants and are always expecting to be on the move again. Financially, I scraped along counting every franc—also a severe restriction on social life. In spite of the friendly apartment at St Paul, I felt by this time acutely isolated, dependent almost entirely for company on the folk who congregated in the café of the Studios Wacker after class each day. And although I felt far more at one with my fellow dancers and less of an oddball, I never have, and did not then, find the dance world a stimulating or particularly congenial place. My closest friends were almost always girls who read and passed me on books, and who had some attitudes which were not the one-dimensional product of ballet life.

I detect a bending-over-backwards hesitancy to say what I really feel, but since it is implicit in what I write such soft-peddling is slightly ridiculous. I was, quite simply, too mentally alert not to have been bored out of my mind by this kind of existence, with a feeling of being dulled by my experiences, and, I think, a deep resentment building up over this dulling. At the back of my mind sounded words my father had once said: 'Between the age of sixteen and twenty-two are the years when a person is at their most receptive to ideas and experiences.' Without labouring the question of his exact correctness over the timespan, the basic point is important. The years of late adolescence and early adulthood

170

are, or should be, years of opening up, a period of vigorous mental playtime, a time to try out new ideas and ideologies and lifestyles. And if disruptions ensue they are not half so traumatic as the enormous personal upheavals that occur when people attempt to make radical changes later in their lives. It's a time when life should be illumined by a large gleaming question mark, not coffined by sameness and routine and a sense of being unable to escape.

I had got myself trapped. I didn't know how to move forwards or how to get out, and to that extent the ballet life had become as monotonous as a treadmill. I did not know how to disengage myself from the repetitive pattern of half-promised work, dashed hopes, and occasional reward which is in itself an excellent conditioning for clinging to the *status quo*. According to one of the classic deconditioning experiments in behaviourist psychology, it was the pigeons—or rats—who had sometimes been rewarded, sometimes not, who took the longest to be trained out of their original response. So, like some victim of applied Skinnerian theory, I hung on and on.

Had there been anyone to talk to, anyone to whom I could have started to unburden, it might have helped me to realise that I had a major problem to face—just as in London at the time of my injured foot I had had one to face. It was, of course, the same problem, coming round for the second time. I was not going to make it as a distinguished dancer, and although this knowledge was contained most of the time by a kind of dull suppression, occasionally it surfaced in a fit of something like despair. It is a measure of my isolation that the only person who witnessed any of my unhappiness was an elderly Russian gentleman, white-haired and dapper, who lived in the same street as myself, little more than a nodding acquaintance. One bleak evening I met him at the little local grocery where we were both doing our shopping. I had a streaming cold and was feeling so miserable that he immediately insisted I should come up to his flat where he would dose me with something for my cold. The something turned out to be a fiery alcoholic drink which, combined with his solicitude, soon had me sobbing out my woes in a long incoherent stream—about how beautiful ballet could be and how I longed to be a beautiful dancer and knew I never would, and how failed and wretched I felt. Dear man, he treated me like a little girl, and mopped my nose for me and put his arm round my shoulders and kissed me tenderly and a little greedily. But my great tale of heartbreak only provoked him to roars of laughter, and a fairy godfather benevolence which assured me that the sun would shine again and I would be happy. All he saw was a small child with a broken toy, touching but comical.

There was certainly that element, but there was also a deep sense of rejection, just like being spurned by a lover or being found spiritually unworthy, melodramatic words, perhaps, but I hope not unique to my own experience of artistic disillusion. I hope to share it with anyone who has had the painful experience of reassessing their talent in a downward direction. The other disillusion, of course, is with the object of faith (or love) itself, which is also crumbling. Something is becoming 'not worth the effort'. And indeed, from the time I was sixteen I had had my doubts whether ballet was really an art form worthy of my total personal commitment. About so much of it there was a relentless triviality, disguised by the spectacular quality of the physical skills involved. Although a ballet dancer, I was by no means one hundred per cent balletomane.

Another thing that kept me abroad was the thought of returning to Edinburgh. In spite of the joyless face Paris presented at this time, it was, nonetheless, a cosmopolitan city. It was the Big World. It was Europe, and it breathed European history and culture even if by this time I walked its boulevards and passed its monuments unnoticing. Without ever having substantiated this feeling of attraction towards European culture, as distinct from British, by any intensive study, it was important to me. At a groping schoolgirl level I knew that Paris was in the mainstream of Western history and civilisation, that it had the vitality that comes from being part of a landmass, at times stretching its own self far across the map, at times shrunk back and overrun, cultures intermingling through force as well as peaceable means in a way that fails to happen for an insular nation.

Yet at heart I remained quite pathetically British, not knowing how to make the transition from a kind of well-meaning decency of behaviour, with its attendant ideology of ill-thought-out humanitarianism to the crisper, more cynical mode of French interaction, with its implication of defiant cultural assertion. Most of non-Communist Europe now suffers from some degree of jaded disillusion with itself, Britain included. But in the early 1950s, I doubt if it had percolated through from the circles of the intellectual élite (if indeed that is where such trends start) to affect the ideology of the man in the street. And the French man or woman in the street seemed, despite the humiliation of wartime occupation, remarkably resilient. Moreover, there was as yet little sign of the ghastly uniformity of the global village—which has done nothing to spread individual cultures wider but simply smeared a common-denominator transatlantic message through identical media across the European map. So, even as I was being slowly defeated by the situation, there remained a lingering exhilaration at the fact of going it alone in the middle of Europe.

This challenge made me fiercely reluctant to ask my parents for help, especially in the matter of paying for journeys back home. Not to be able to get myself back under my own steam seemed the final humiliation—a kind of ignominious repatriation. In one letter asking for funds for this purpose I assured them that I was not going to be all my life a 'sensitive scrounger'. This, I am sure, was entirely self-concocted. My parents never showed the slightest reluctance to bail me out. But, in the way of people who are basically very dependent but too proud to admit it, I went to the other extreme to 'prove' something. Attempting to prove something about oneself is, of all preoccupations, the most futile. It only leads to obsessional re-entry into situations which revive all the original feelings of inadequacy. People do accomplish quite remarkable things under this impulse, but usually at a rather hideous cost to themselves and others. It is a truism to point out that 'proof' is never convincing for very long.

The fact remains that even if I could be put back in time to my nineteen-year-old self I doubt if I would discover any more clearly what were my 'true' feelings about the situation. The question that needed posing—whether to carry on dancing, and if not, what then to do—was buried away under layers of protective horror at this threat to my sense of self. I had, after all, spent half of my life involved with dance. There was no other 'me'. Even the shadowy speculative person who had kept the journal going for so many years had been abandoned and forgotten, disowned, perhaps. So I continued to drift.

Germany and After

The opening days of the German tour were like rain after drought, the long-awaited oasis in the desert, or, more appropriately, a fair wind after being becalmed, for it was the zestful feeling of being in action, not lying back in idleness, that was wanted to put heart into us.

In view of the fact that horizons seemed to be expanding, with a new and apparently enthusiastic financial backer, the repertoire had been freshened up with two revivals, both works by David Lichine. One was *La Rencontre,* his stylised rendering of the meeting between Oedipus and the Sphinx; the other *Aubade,* was also on a classical theme, the killing of Acteon by the goddess Diana and her nymphs, and its elegant choreography was set to Poulenc's music. I enjoyed dancing in both of these, particularly as one of the Sphinx's three attendants, who act as kind of trainers preparing her for the trial of strength.

The first new ballet for two years was created by Ruth Page, an American choreographer, a frippery piece of nonsense called *Impromptu au Bois* to Ibert's *Divertissements,* a piece of music I still can't hear without detestation. We all loathed the new work, but at least it was kitted out with attractive costumes made by the best theatrical costumier in Paris, and that in itself gave a mild uplift. I thought of Ruth Page as a rich American dilettante. Moneyed she certainly seemed to be—I think she personally undertook the entire costs of productions—but to my surprise, I find she has quite a long and honourable mention in at least two encyclopaedias of dance. It does not change my view of her as a fairly banal choreographer, though, to be fair, this dreadful little ballet and another longer work she put on for us later in the year are all that I have to go on.

South Germany, where our tour started, was a delicious sight. It was springtime, and I was struck by a strong sense of cleanliness about the place and the prettiness of it, despite the scars and gaps in the towns from their wartime battering. Nevertheless, living standards—as we met them in hotels and restaurants and shops—were high and, compared to France, inexpensive. We all started making happy calculations about what we could buy with our new-found touring wealth. The company was dancing well. We were popular and successful. It was all starting to swing. For the first time for months, dancing had regained some of its old pleasure and excitement. And then— once again I was laid low. A slight inflammation on my heel refused to die down and instead spread with sinister speed to my ankle where I developed another huge abscess which completely prevented me from putting my foot to the ground, let alone dancing. I wept copiously in disappointment, but there was nothing for it. I had to be left behind in Frankfurt after going to only half a dozen of the scheduled fourteen towns, and missed out on the high spot of the tour, which was a performance in West Berlin.

But by this time I was far too preoccupied with pain to feel miserable at being thus abandoned, and thankful that I was receiving medical attention at the hands of the British Army whom someone in the company administration must have contacted to produce a doctor. An exceedingly young, round-faced medic on national service turned up one day at my hotel—where, incidentally, the man at the reception desk had said pleasantly, seeing the home address on my passport, 'Edinburgh—ah yes! I bombed it', as if this forged some friendly social bond between us. The young doctor, having pondered over my leg, decided that the abscess must be lanced, which he proceeded to do the next day. It's an experience I would rather not repeat, for a quick squirt of surface freezing did nothing at all to blunt the sensations of the knife, or the prolonged probing around inside the incision which followed.

After that ordeal the worst was over. I hobbled around on the arm of the young doctor, when I was not being driven in the countryside, or taken to the officers' mess where he introduced me with charming pride as 'my ballerina'. I was even recovered enough to enjoy some night life and being inconsequentially in love with my saviour.

This private catastrophe was parallelled by a hammer blow which had fallen yet again on that unfortunate ballet company, whose best efforts to raise its fortunes could never prevail against some irreversible thumbs-down sign which destiny seemed to have signalled. When the rest returned from Berlin, I was told the news. Our promising new impresario had gone bankrupt. The rest of the performances were cancelled, and he was trying to avoid paying us for them. But after two days of battling between him and the massed forces of our administrator, ballet master, chef d'orchestre, and a friendly lawyer, this money at least was extorted. Meanwhile, the prospects of touring South America, supposedly to follow, once more dwindled to a tiny star about to go out, like the last fall of a Roman candle.

Sadly we returned to Paris. There was only one other brief engagement in sight, a three-day visit to Palermo in Sicily. It was by now mid-June and powerfully hot, and our visit coincided with a flower festival in which we took part, a crazy idea, but presumably to give ourselves some publicity. For two and a half hours we were trailed round the streets on a float, wearing classical long tutus which left us exposed from the bust upwards to the powerful rays of the afternoon sun. By the evening, I and one or two other fair skins were running mild temperatures and someone obligingly swabbed down my burnt arms and neck with a kind of salad-dressing of oil and vinegar. 'The mob were so excited by the belles of the Ballets des Champs Elysées,' I wrote home rather sarcastically 'that we had to have police in strong numbers to push us a way through to the theatre'.

I knew by now that I was on my way home and probably for good. The beautiful calm sail from Palermo to Naples, lit first by a glorious sunset and then by a moonrise which evoked every dreamy romantic association in poetry or music, was the first leg of our journey back to Paris, but I was not going to pause there longer than to make arrangements about forwarding my trunk, a decisive step. 'Paris is not a particularly pleasant place when one has nothing to do and not much money,' I admitted at last to my parents.

The exhaustion which must have been part of the cause of that abscess was by no means dissipated by the enforced rest I had had for the best part of a month before going to Sicily. During the few days in Paris before that trip I slept hours and hours on end, day and night, heavy unrefreshing sleep which left me feeling as if I had been drugged. It- became embarrassing. I was staying with Alex whose temperament of brittle nervous energy could not understand such lethargy. She called it 'unnatural', and I started to feel like a sleep-freak, battled hard to stay awake, but always had to give in.

I also had to give in over the matter of my homeward fare, 'Do you expect me to sell the suit off my back to get you to London?' said Monsieur Robin with gesticulating indignation when I asked for money for this purpose. It had been a long shot, and once again my parents stumped up.

I travelled home, feeling as I always did on these journeys, untidy, slightly grubby and, out of the context of my dance companions, a bit of a tinker compared with all the fresh young holidaymakers around me. Such clothes as I possessed were limp and tired, like their owner, from constant use and frequent travel. Enviously I looked at another young girl in the train compartment, a French Algerian, as pretty and toothsome as a nicely browned biscuit, with her smooth tan, bouncing curls and impeccable grey costume. We were joined by a dark-haired young Englishman and his sister, and the four of us had a merry companionable journey continued on the ferry where the French Algerian girl looked even more laughingly attractive and windswept, her curls blowing in the sharp cross-channel wind. I was certain that Tim would immediately fall for her, but to my surprise, it was between him and myself that vibrations set up which later developed into my first real consummated love-affair some months later. And for once luck was on my side. I had chosen, or been chosen, by one of the sunniest, most charming, life-loving men I have ever met in my life. He was, in fact, too nice for me, too gentle to be able to cope with the storms of anger which my dissatisfaction with life tended to brew up, too optimistic (and protected) to understand the introspective misery which I used to stew in, as I contemplated the morass of fallen hopes and frustrated artistry in which I seemed to be eternally stuck.

For in spite of my intention I was not yet finished with the ballet. With the perversity of a ghost that will not be laid, I had hardly had time to get home after the Sicilian trip, draw breath, and start facing the question 'What next?' when, to my astonishment, the company surfaced again in the form of a letter announcing that a month's season in London had been fixed. I was not at all pleased. But it would have taken far more resolution than I could muster to step out now, when the company was coming almost to my doorstep, and my parents were tingling with excitement at the idea of being able to watch me perform.

What they saw should have shown them, if nothing else, which way the wind was blowing. I was not the dancer who had left home. I might have gained a little stage-craft, but I had lost most of my main artistic charms, quickness, fluidity, lyrical quality. I was exhausted and it showed. For once, and for reasons best known to himself, my father held back on forthright, honest criticism. Apparently, my parents and myself could not confront each other across the sad fact that the dance venture was failing. As though powerless to break away, I returned for a final round in Paris with the company.

Autumn again. But I have no recollection of exhilaration, no memory of being stirred by the bustle of falling bronzed leaves, the crisp sharpness of September air, the excitement of Paris invigorated and on the tracks again after the somnolent disintegration of August and late summer. For the first time I was not staying in either a hotel or a pension, but in a tiny flat which

Alex's mother owned and had agreed to rent to me for a very low sum.

It was a grim little dungeonette of a place—except that unlike a dungeon, this place was on the seventh floor, and being a *chambre de bonne* had to be reached by the back stairway where there was no lift. It had one tiny room, with an even tinier cupboard-like space off it with the usual ancient alarming gas contraption for heating dribbles of water, and some kind of cooking stove. I can't think that even the French were careless enough of hygiene to put a lavatory beside the cooker, so that must have been somewhere along the corridor. It was a spooky, gloomy little place, and perhaps it is as well that we spent so much time in the theatre rehearsing and performing that I had little leisure to contemplate its limitations, which I had not a spare sou to spend on improving.

In spite of the odd flutter of pleasure, like chance visitors from the homeland, and a few outings with French student friends, life got steadily grimmer. We were by this time in the middle of a season in a theatre in the Avenue Wagram, not our old base at the Champs Elysées theatre. It was receiving a good press, but was stretching us all to our limits—and still no sign of our pay. Ruth Page had mounted another ballet, *La Revanche,* to the music of Verdi's *Il Trovatore.* We turned up our noses at this one too, but the designs were by Clavé, one of the leading stage designers at the time, and the production was fairly sumptuous. Two of Ballet Rambert's choreographers, Walter Gore and Frank Staff, had also been invited over to create ballets, which we were learning and rehearsing as the season was in progress.

I should have realised by the fact that I was so delighted when English folk started appearing on the scene how dismally homesick I was becoming. Tim's appearance for a week of sexual happiness, which was rather extraordinary given our mutual lack of experience, only aggravated my unhappiness once he'd gone. I was by this time extremely depressed, and starting to show various signs of having reached the end of my tether. Instead of getting hardened to living poor, which by now I'd been doing for some time, I found it more and more humiliating, perhaps because my *chambre de bonne* was in a well-to-do *quartier.* Shopping for minute amounts of groceries, sometimes on tick, sometimes paid with bottles on which there was a deposit, fitted well enough into downtrodden areas where others were doing the same. But in affluent central Paris it was an exposure from which I flinched.

I got drunk far too easily—not that there were so many opportunities, but I went on one notable binge in the full knowledge that there was an evening performance ahead. No matter—my cousin was passing through Paris on his way to West Africa, and with rioting recklessness we hit the town, starting at lunchtime and continuing throughout the afternoon. I turned up at the theatre (having procured him from somewhere a seat for the performance) utterly and completely sloshed.

What followed was pure fall-about comedy, except that by the grace of God I did not actually measure my length on stage. Unbelieving, the other girls in the dressing-room watched while I staggered in, sang and laughed and carried on a conversation with myself, and stirred not a finger to put on my make-up, get warmed up, or put on my costume. Finally, with a few minutes to go, giggling incredulously, they took over, daubed my face with some grease-paint, threaded my flaccid limbs into tights and shoes, and zipped me into my costume. Some drunkard's sanity prompted me to warn my partner that he would have to provide an exceedingly strong steady arm, but that was in the second ballet. For the first, I swayed terror-struck in the wings while the music played inexorably on towards my entry, which was alone and unaided. The stage yawned in front of me, vast as the Sahara; somewhere a day's ride away a light shone brightly. But conditioning is a powerful thing. Aiming in the general direction of that light I launched myself on stage, crossing it *en diagonal,* my legs unfolding and bending at approximately the right moments. Being on point felt like trying to dance on two tiny pins, and the length and extension of my limbs was an inconstant datum, but somehow I got through that ballet without catastrophe, and indeed the next, though I was still so drunk that turning a double pirouette in front of my partner—who fortunately clapped his hands like a vice round my waist as I came to rest—felt as though the whole universe had become a mad roundabout. The experience was one of acute physical terror.

After *le vin gai* follows *le vin triste.* My bravura snapped suddenly and there followed the inevitable storm of tears. I sobbed helplessly with my head on, of all people's, Ruth Page's shoulder. God knows what I told her but it produced screams of unmistakeably motherly laughter. She patted me and petted me and called me by all sorts of endearments, and a sudden gush of warm good feeling flowed into what had been till then a wary and unenthusiastic relationship. The next time I met her, sober and buttoned back inside my hostile reserve, she tried to tell me that that drunken evening had been the first time she had felt able to get 'close' to me and realise what a 'sweet girl' I was underneath. I eyed her coldly, feeling an extra layer of constraint imposing itself. Something was very far wrong if I could only be spontaneous when I was paralytic with drink.

I did a little anxious checking up about my performance that night, and asked one of the company members who had been watching out front whether he'd noticed anything amiss. 'No,' he said, surprised. 'I thought you were in extra good form. You had a smile which hit the back of the stalls.'

The next unseemly incident was less amusing, and involved a row royal with my landlady, Alex's mother, an anxious uptight little woman whose years of living in France had done nothing to shift her Cockney whine. She came one evening into the dressing-room to collect the last month's rent, 5,000 francs (about £5). By exquisite and unbearable irony we had that very day, after a campaign of furious collective pestering and threats of mutiny extorted exactly that sum each from the management. The worst humiliation of all was to be made to feel, as we were, that this was some kind of bounty being extended to us, instead of a fraction of what was due to us from the past exhausting weeks. I had had barely two hours in which to taste the sense of relief that I was in funds, at least for the next short while, overlooking the fact that the rent was due, before Madame appeared demanding it.

I asked her to give me a little longer, explained that this was the first pay we had seen in weeks, but she was adamant. At that I lost my head and my temper beyond any hope of recall. I screamed at her for being an avaricious heartless money-grubber, flung the precious 5,000 franc note on the floor in front of her, and carried on like a runaway train hurtling down the tracks of hysteria. The dressing-room inhabitants were pale and aghast. Even by Gallic standards this scene was staggering. Since it was conducted in English they had only the intensity and the violence of the emotions to guide them, and the exchange, if it could be called that, of money. Unfairly, but not surprisingly, their sympathies were on my side. All they saw was precious money being torn like a living member from one of their comrades in need. But I was not going to let Madame have it without extorting *my* price. The note lay like a kind of challenge between us, and knowing I was going to lose it, I turned the tables on our own recent humiliation at the hands of the management with a vengeance. I made her look foolish and unpleasant; I sneered at her meanness, making it sound as indecent as I knew how, and of course eventually she had to stoop to pick up the money, an act full of echoes of grovelling and grubbing. It was an ugly end to a very ugly scene.

This kind of outburst was only one sign of the collective strain and ill-feeling which was getting a grip of the company. It was a poisonous time, the only period with the ballet that makes unalleviated bad remembering. The rest had often been stressful in the extreme, but the dispiriting theme of the downward slide had been well ornamented with incidentals—either places or people or events which supplied light relief or amusement or even healthy counter-irritation. This final season in Paris was like being sucked underground into some cave-like existence in which we never saw the light of day. We spent our life in the theatre. When we weren't performing we were rehearsing for a change of programme, or fighting for our money. My bleak little flat, handily near, became simply a comfortless extension to the theatre. We were fed up with each other, fed up with the eternal double-talk about money, and the fact that in spite of a good season there still didn't seem to be any. We loathed and distrusted Jean Robin, with the helpless loathing of puppets for their puppeteer, a suitable if banal metaphor for dancers.

I cannot help wondering whether this man's persistence, applauded in almost every newspaper as an act of courage, wasn't in fact some kind of diseased obsession which was now affecting us all. Monsieur Robin never gave any outward sign of being a disinterested, or even particularly interested, lover of the arts. He was simply an administrator with a liking for control. He had no charm or charisma of personality, in fact he was not unlike Nixon— he did not know when the chips were down. What Robin's motives or needs were in keeping the company alive I cannot guess, but by this time his tenacity had reached pathological proportions. We were being squeezed dry, and driven mildly crazy.

I started to feel like a sort of muttering ghost of my former self, except that there was no very clear sense of continuity or connectedness with any former self. I also started to hate myself violently, the only available target to blame for this sense of *gâchis*—that most expressive French word, meaning 'spoiltness'—about my life. I didn't believe I would ever be able to get a job with another company. I would probably have sold my soul to any wizard who could magic away all memory trace of every battement, plié or arabesque I had ever done. And yet I still wanted to hide behind the now tottering façade. Arnold Haskell came over to Paris, saw our performance, and took me out to dinner, obviously rather shocked by my appearance and general state of being. 'You are glad I helped you get over here, aren't you?' he asked anxiously. I don't remember exactly how I replied, but it was certainly not in revelation of the dried-out emptiness within. And somehow the BBC managed to contact me and asked me to script myself a little talk on being a dancer in Paris, which I did—a droll little account of the ups and downs of life which I put over as a kind of picturesque lark. And even added in a touch of sentimental gratitude to my old teacher, Marjorie

Middleton, whom, if I could, I would probably at that point have kicked through a wall for having got me involved in the first place.

After Paris, we went over to North Africa for a fortnight, and after that we came back to Paris, and sat one evening in a café, the whole company, including Walter Gor, Paula Hinton and Frank Staff, to discuss whether to continue. For me, it was at last merely an academic question. I was leaving. Paris was Paris no longer, it was simply a city where life had become too tough by half. I couldn't get out of it fast enough.

Epilogue

I arrived home wanting only one thing, to give up dancing. What I should do with my life, I had absolutely no idea. It was Christmas time, and I got a temporary job serving in a department store to earn some money. I looked and felt terrible—anaemic, puffy, and still liable to erupt in boils. And I was dismally depressed, to such an extent that I imagine I should nowadays have been declared officially 'ill'. Not that that is necessarily helpful, but I badly needed some recognition that, temporarily, I was beaten. I still think—not quite as calmly as I should—that my parents were quite amazingly blind to the state I was in.

I also find it difficult to keep calm when I think of my inability to think or act for myself. At the age of nearly twenty, with two and a half years of the tough world behind me, I was still as dependent as a baby on the judgment of my mother and father over matters affecting my life. So, when my mother implored me not to give up ballet but to have another try, I gave in, though I had no heart for the matter.

Reluctantly I went to London and started training again. But this time there were too many distractions—boyfriends, visits to Oxford where my brother was completing his final year. I was suddenly confronted with the lovely idle make-believe world of upper-class student life, with its balls and Eights Week and cricket matches—and would have liked nothing better than to turn myself into one of the countless china-faced girls who dawdled so prettily in the streets and college gardens on their weekend visits.

Unfortunately, I lacked certain vital qualifications such as spending money, placid nerves, and ignorance of anything outside the correct social set. Instead I was hard up, eking out my allowance with part-time clerking at the Coal Board, had a pulse rate which topped the hundred mark and a tremor of the hands which made people stare. I also felt myself somewhat shopsoiled with experiences which any self-respecting class member would consider rather infra dig.

However unsuitable the model I chose to emulate, it did achieve one thing. I made up my mind to leave ballet once and for all and returned to Edinburgh to face my mother.

I don't think she can have had any idea of the power she wielded. Her angry despair was more than I could cope with. I had robbed her of something precious, deliberately killed off her dearest dreams. Before I had even got inside the front door, she greeted me with the passionate declaration that she could never watch ballet again in her life. She was in tears. I was paralysed with guilt, and accepted without protest that I had forfeited my right to an artistic 'persona', or any of the favours and dispensations that went with it. From henceforth I was absolutely ordinary, must be like other girls, and find something useful to do. The 'something useful' turned out to be a secretarial training, her decision. I acquiesced, neither glad nor sorry. I could think of no alternative except to go to Oxford, like my brother, which was out of the question.

What my mother started, my former teacher continued in the process of demoralisation. 'In other words,' said Marjorie drily when I had finished telling her my doubts and increasing disillusion with both ballet and my own work, 'you've funked it.' Presumably she too was unaware of the lasting impact of her words. For, in spite of my fortitude in coping with the life of a touring dancer, I recognised a fatal germ of truth in what she said. I had shrunk back from engaging some essential part of myself. I had tried to keep hidden both emotion and sensuality, which I found so threatening, in work as I had in living. I had tried to preserve myself as a kind of innocent in both spheres. At her words all sorts of complex spectres threatened to rise. I pushed them down with the strength of panic. Let nobody persuade me I must expose any part of myself again in public.

The only person who seemed to feel sadness on my behalf was my father. I never felt that he loved me or valued me any the less for quitting, and he tried with great tenderness to try and put my mind at rest about the money spent on my career—wasted, I felt, each extra £5 which I'd asked for while I was abroad pressing deep into my conscience. And here again I experience a prickle of unspent emotion. Part of me feels that in her place I too might have acted like my disappointed mother and looked on the whole thing as a rotten investment. Yet another part of me feels like protesting angrily at having taken on that burden of guilt. My health and morale had been badly hammered. I had been put very young into situations which were enough to try older and tougher people. And I had for years provided a window onto a world, half fantasy, half real, which had supplied all manner of diversions and delights. I suppose it was the loss of this, and the strangely important sense that she had a child that was doing something 'different', that so upset my mother. But I still find the harshness which lies at the bottom of most kinds of love a chilling phenomenon.

Leaving ballet raised so many painful issues and such confusion that I refused to face any of it. I buried the whole thing, unresolved, along with any part of myself that had aesthetic hungers or expressive needs. As for emotion, I was more than ever convinced how strong and dangerous a thing it was, and this too I did my misguided best to banish. One thing which haunted me was the half knowledge that I would not get away with these evasions, and that some time I would be forced to face the dread of exposure in some creative form again.

Whether the disastrous marriage I made at the age of twenty-one was a way of ensuring the greatest distance from that threat, I don't know, for of all my adult actions it remains the most incredible, as well as the most inaccessible to memory. I can only make guesses as to why, in a spirit of Russian roulette, I allowed that particularly unsuitable suitor to win out over several more

188

appealing. He was melancholy and reserved, a doctor by profession and scarcely interested in the arts. His own source of poetry, from which he was largely cut off, was the wild sodden landscapes of the West Highlands and the Outer Hebrides, where one side of his family originated. To me it had zero appeal, and added to the primitive fear this strange man aroused in me, along with my reluctant pity. He had a pronounced chip on his shoulder, a childhood and adolescence scarred with serious chest illness, and, I later discovered, a drink problem. Although I think I felt some relief at his understanding of the sombre side of life, compared to the brittle cheerful inexperience of most of my age-mates, I was not at all in love with him, and only pretended to be in order to give some credibility to the engagement.

I know it is not uncommon for women to throw themselves into destructive partnerships in a mistaken attempt to sort out their lives. But such a piece of obstinate craziness as mine—I was not interested in housewifery, wept at the thought of being under virtual house arrest as a GPs wife, didn't want children—must have drawn on other and more twisted motives. Put clinically, I think I was experiencing a quite serious schizoid depression, despite outward appearances of popularity and party-going. Put figuratively, I envisage some angry schemer in my unconscious, some deeply self-destructive element determined to kill off any part of me that dared to respond to leisure or light-heartedness.

Whatever the cause, I felt powerless to pull back. And what I entered into was in all conscience a sad enough existence. My husband was a man imbued with a kind of despair, whose origins I never completely understood. It may have been in part an aftermath of the Korean War, which as a national service RAF doctor based in India he had experienced through being flown in to attend to casualties. A leading journalist once commented to me that those involved with that particlar war had had specially acute problems of 're-entry' into normal society. Nobody wanted to know about it, we were all too busy trying to forget World War II. Perhaps for Hugh, his own personal traumas of illness—he was invalided out of the RAF with yet more lung trouble—were fatally exacerbated by that encounter with disorganised violence, in which men were sent out criminally under-equipped for the conditions they had to face, while back home there was hardly a ripple in the collective conscience.

I am not in a position to say, for he tended not to talk freely about his experiences. All I know is that like so many of his countrymen he could not bear to face his own tremendous vulnerability, and tried to forget it in drink. And that, in its turn, changed him from a caring and clinically acute medical practitioner into an apathetic and disillusioned time-server. He was, I will not deny, a terrible man to be married to, but when he died in an accident which had more than a whiff of death-wish about it the shock and sense of loss was appalling. This is not the place to expand on the extraordinary bonds which the sharing of home and children forge between two ill-matched people. All that needs to be said is that I was, for a while, devastated by his death.

But one cannot bury a certain kind of energy, a certain kind of passion, for ever. The very turmoil of this sudden tragedy and its aftermath seemed to produce a kind of explosion of need in me to be doing something—writing, drawing, singing—anything at all which would put me in touch with that buried bit of self. The timing of this personal renaissance was exquisitely bad. In society's eyes, and those of my own conscience, it was frivolous and arbitrary to be pining after creative endeavour when the fate of two very small children was at stake. Yet pine I did, and although the children did come first then and for many years, I tried as best I could to combine looking after them and their needs with some dabblings in my own directions, as well as either studying for a degree or holding down a job.

I also tried to give my children a more varied upbringing than I myself had had, but this did not go down too well. They would really have preferred a plump comfortable cushion of a mother, not someone restless and mildly unorthodox like myself; and although my son used loyally to swear that I was much more fun than his schoolmates' squarely upholstered matriarchs, I think they sensed all too acutely the lack of security of their position as the offspring of a single rather strange parent.

I also craved security. Yet time and again the inner battle broke out—between my responsible parental self wanting a place in the social sun for herself and her children, and the artistic venturer, still unhatched and afraid, but pecking away for permission to be allowed to try and refind that vital dimension of poetry in life. For to me poetry is not simply one art form; it is a mode of experience and the raw material of all art.

My life continued for many years to be 99 per cent prosaic. There were flashes of poetry—singing lessons, sculpture classes, and the joy of setting up my own diminutive sculpting studio at home. There were also love affairs. But for the most part I continued to stare discontentedly out of my university room where I was supposed to be probing sociological theory (the outcome of taking an honours degree), and later to stare out equally sullenly from the anonymous fortress of a civil service building.

Perhaps my forays into different art forms were the means of keeping some sparks of desire alive. But I think a key move in the struggle to see daylight again was taken when I started, once again, to keep a journal. At one stage this was nothing more than 'dear diary' introspection. But gradually it changed in character and became a mixture of personal feelings and writer's notebook. Language I discovered had the power to create and recreate. Like Anais Nin, I started to substantiate my otherwise unconvincing existence through its use.

It wasn't enough, by itself. Nor was the fact that I had started getting regularly into print as a feature-writer. (It was, ironically, dance that provided the initial opening into journalism when I was asked to review a ballet for the *Scotsman* newspaper.) When I decided to try and write seriously a few years ago, I realised that I had no solid personal ground to stand on. For more than twenty crowded years my life appeared to have been lived by someone else. 'I,' for the most part, had been someone responding to necessity, borrowed motivations, others' expectations, or some censorious monitor in my own head. There had been patches that felt real, of course, but they were only patches. I had no proper territory. It was a bad discovery to make, for I felt, intuitively, what I later found put into words by John Fowles—the necessity for a writer to be able to roam freely through his or her past, for the whole thing to be there to be drawn upon directly or indirectly. Slowly I had to concede what I had no wish to concede—that the 'real past' stopped for me at the point where I gave up dancing. Before that, people were rounded and alive. I had no difficulty in believing in their existence. Afterwards, too many memories of people and events have the quality of bad art or bad living—forced, strained and unconvincing.

Another evil legacy of those years was that I no longer trusted myself to tell the difference between wanting to do something and wanting to play a certain role. The middle-class disease. Only most members would not see it as a disease, for one of their most cherished beliefs is that going through the motions, if done with sufficient finesse, is as good as, if not indistinguishable, from real experience. Towards the whole business I have the violent antipathy of the reformed alcoholic to drink. Nevertheless, in a fit of deep discouragement about my progress as a writer, I found myself once more embroiled in questions of 'role'.

I started to think for the first time about the whole question of art and Art, of my own mixed motives as a dancer, of how much of that venture had been coloured by belief in a non-existent ideal called the Artist. Was I still chasing that ridiculous phantom? Still stuck in the belief that there was something holy and mystical about Art? Still trying to cross some boundary which only the philistine belief in 'great artists' and 'ordinary people' would try and draw in the first place? It is childish stuff; but nevertheless for the first time in my Art-worshipping and timidly art-loving life, I was trying, under duress, to come to terms with disillusionment without resorting to the cynical dismissal: 'You're no good'.

Before resolving any of these matters, I went through some

queasy months. I wondered whether giving up secure employment had after all only been a kind of 'dare'—now having very
real and uncomfortable consequences; and whether ending an
important relationship because I found it impossible to combine
with learning to write had been yet another destructive act,
prematurely and hastily done.

These were not good times. But at the end of them, certain bits
of mist had cleared. The capital A had been knocked out of art.
The word 'inspiration' had been replaced by a dictum of bald
practicality: You are either prepared to work hard and believe
that you have ideas to develop, or you are not. As for
'dedication', that I concluded, is a word which others apply to
others, or themselves only in the context of ideological soft-sell on
a public rostrum. I doubt if many people use it in their private
vocabulary.

At last I felt that I'd got past the point where I had stuck as a
dancer; where I'd backed down from the hard task of making
clear to myself something about the nature of artistic
commitment, or commitment of any kind. Inevitably I have asked
myself the question: should I or should I not have carried on
longer in dance? But the answer is not in terms of 'yes' or 'no'; it
is that both alternatives required that I come of age. If I had gone
on, it would have had to be with more real love of dance and less
exclusive love of me, the dancer. If I had got out, it would have
had to be with unashamed sorrow, instead of black rage over
disappointment, and a rational acknowledgement that the high
price of that particular commitment was not one that I was
prepared to pay. Also that defeat is not total dishonour.

I think it was working through that bad patch in my efforts to
develop as a writer that gave me the first real contact with the
person I used to be. It was not the dreadful encounter I had feared.
At long last I seemed able to face my 'teenage self with some
sympathy and without the sense of bitter mutual recrimination
which had flavoured past attempts at dialogue.

It was as good a surprise as returning to Paris. After twenty-
five years I went back on a short working trip, without any

anticipation of what the experience would be like. I felt neutral and curious, that's all, and totally unprepared for the great surge of pure *gladness* at being there again. I'd forgotten that I knew the place so well. I'd forgotten how much I loved it, and completely forgotten how deliriously happy I must sometimes have been for it to hold such friendly excitement now. There was this unique sense of being given a delicious and unexpected present, a slice of forgotten familiarity, a place that felt like mine.

I had never before realised that memories could return intact, still live but purged of their bad associations. I think it is a sign of growing old, or do I simply mean growing up? Whichever, it seems worth commemorating that neither process need be as devastating as one fears. And so I wrote this book as a kind of celebration of rediscovery.